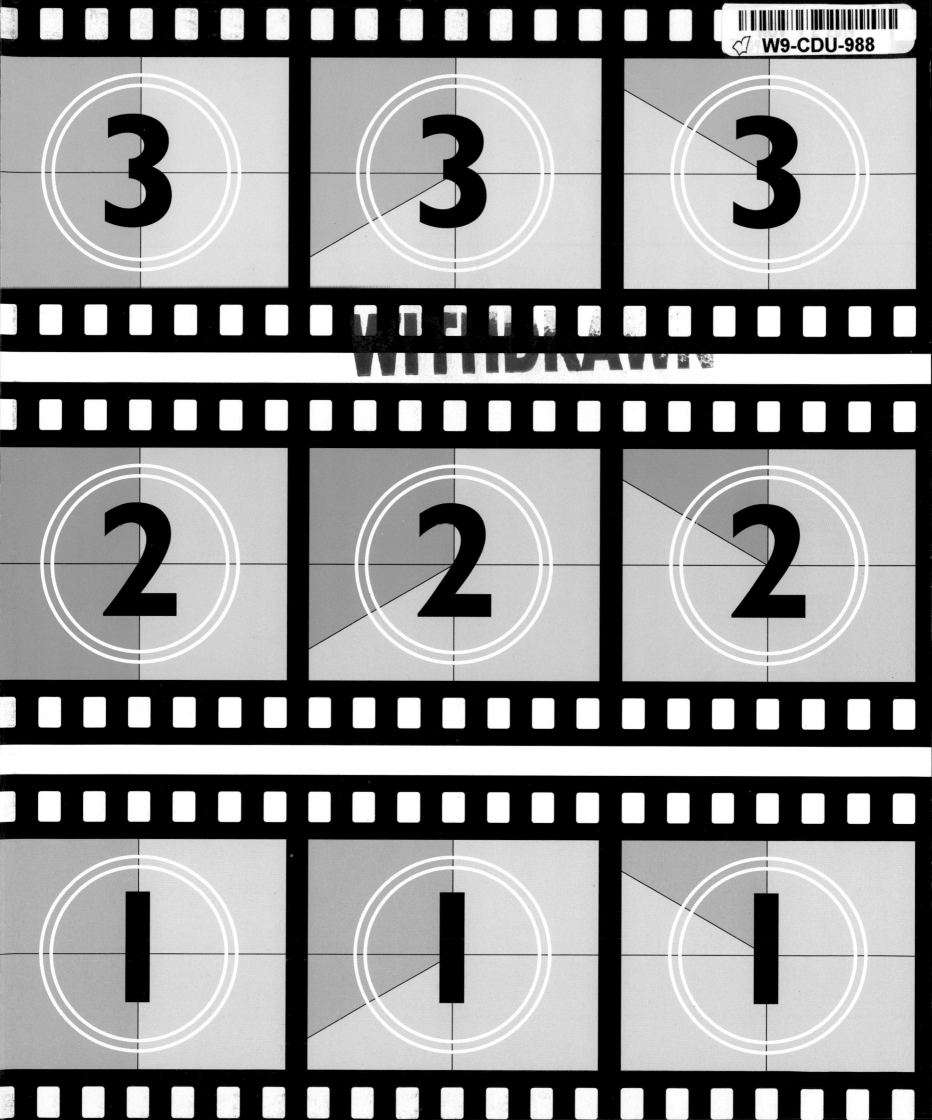

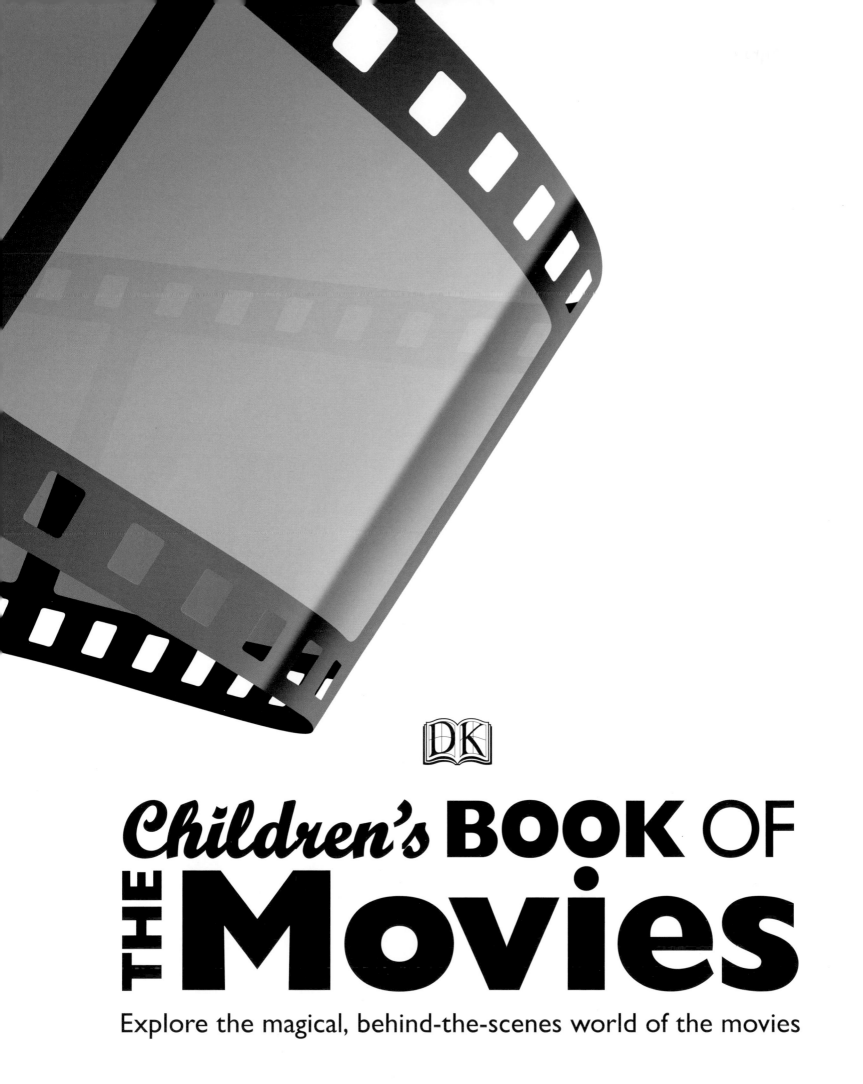

Children's BOOK OF THE Movies

Explore the magical, behind-the-scenes world of the movies

DK

LONDON, NEW YORK, MELBOURNE,
MUNICH, AND DELHI

Project editor Lizzie Munsey
Designer Fiona Macdonald
Editor Ann Baggaley
US editor Margaret Parrish
Producer, preproduction Rachel Ng
Producer Gemma Sharpe
Jacket designer Laura Brim
Jacket editor Manisha Majithia
Managing Editor Paula Regan
Managing Art Editor Owen Peyton Jones
Publisher Sarah Larter
Art Director Phil Ormerod
Associate Publishing Director Liz Wheeler
Publishing Director Jonathan Metcalf

DK Delhi
Senior Art Editor Chhaya Sajwan
Art Editors Neha Sharma, Supriya Mahajan, Nidhi Mehra
Assistant Art Editors Payal Rosalind Malik,
Ankita Mukherjee, Namita
Project Editor Antara Moitra
Assistant Editor Archana Ramachandran
Managing Art Editor Arunesh Talapatra
Managing Editor Pakshalika Jayaprakash
DTP Designers Rajesh Singh Adhikari, Vishal Bhatia,
Umesh Singh Rawat
Pre-production Manager Balwant Singh
Production Manager Pankaj Sharma
Assistant Picture Researcher Ashwin Raju Adimari

FILMCLUB / FILM NATION UK
This book was created in partnership with FILMCLUB
(now part of FILM NATION UK). See **www. filmclub.org**.
Lead Writers Corinna Downing, Kirsten Geekie
Producer Sam Wainstein
Writers Ellen E. Jones, Ben Davies, Harry Harris
Research Kate Rooney and the FILMCLUB team

First published in the United States in 2014 by DK Publishing
4th Floor, 345 Hudson Street, New York, New York

14 15 16 17 18 10 9 8 7 6 5 4 3 2 1
001—192630—Apr/2014

Copyright © 2014 Dorling Kindersley Limited
All rights reserved

Without limiting the rights under copyright reserved above, no part of this
publication may be reproduced, stored in or introduced into a retrieval
system, or transmitted, in any form, or by any means (electronic, mechanical,
photocopying, recording, or otherwise), without the prior written permission
of both the copyright owner and the above publisher of this book.
Published in Great Britain by Dorling Kindersley Limited.

A catalog record for this book is available from the Library of Congress.
ISBN 978-1-4654-1662-9

DK books are available at special discounts when purchased in bulk for
sales promotions, premiums, fund-raising, or educational use. For details,
contact: DK Publishing Special Markets, 4th floor, 345 Hudson Street,
New York, New York 10014 or SpecialSales@dk.com.

The theme or content of some movies listed in *Children's
Book of the Movies* may not be suitable for all children. Please check the
film's rating and consider its suitability before letting your child view it.

Printed and bound by Leo Paper Products, China
Discover more at
www.dk.com

Contents

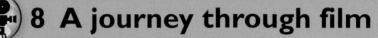

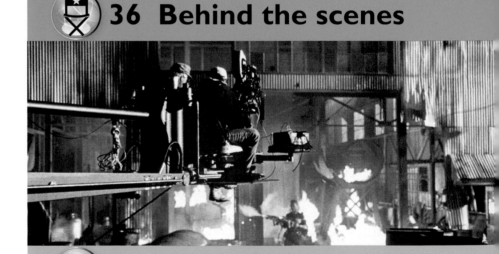

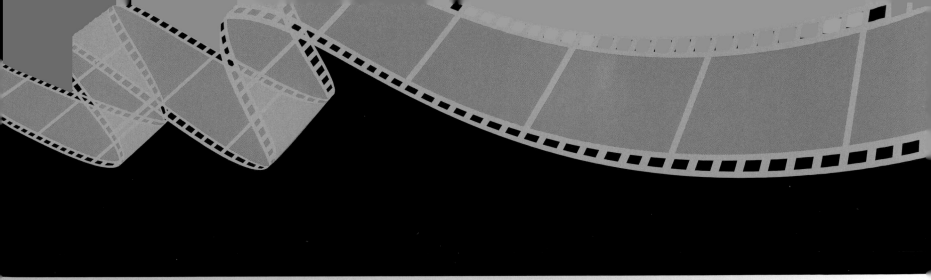

◄ The Wicked Witch hides from Dorothy in *The Wizard of Oz* (1939).

◄ A camera operator and director use a crane to capture the perfect shot.

◄ The animals try to get back to New York, in *Madagascar 3: Europe's Most Wanted* (2012).

A journey through **film**

Movies have changed a lot since they were first made in black-and-white with no sound— modern movies have **color, sound, and special effects, and some are even in 3-D**.

The story of the movies

The first moving images were shown to audiences in the 1800s. Since then, **new technologies and storytelling techniques** have developed, different film styles have gone in and out of fashion, and audience tastes have changed. One important thing has stayed the same—we still love going to the movies.

An early film projector

The birth of the movies

A series of inventions led up to the first recorded moving image in the late 1800s. Earlier machines could show films to only one person at a time, but it was when the Lumière brothers projected a movie for an audience in 1895 that the movies were born.

Invented in 1882, the "camera gun" could take 12 pictures in a second.

Telling stories

Recorded images were first used by scientists, but in the 1900s they became entertainment for everyone. In France, Georges Méliès made fantastical films such as *A Trip to the Moon* (1902). The first permanent movie theater, the "Nickelodeon," opened in the US in 1905.

French filmmaker Georges Méliès

The silent era

The first movie audiences watched movies with no sound. While silent comedian Charlie Chaplin tickled audiences, Disney's cartoon character Mickey Mouse made his debut in *Steamboat Willie* (1928).

Talkies

From the 1930s, movies with sound became the norm. In the West, new film styles like musicals provided an escape for audiences during the hardship of the Great Depression. In China, films about real-life problems were more popular.

Audrey Hepburn in *Funny Face* (1957)

Age of realism

As the world came to terms with World War II, so did the movies, with films like *A Matter of Life and Death* (1946, right) about a British Air Force pilot. In Italy, many film studios were destroyed in the war, and filmmaking on the streets became popular.

The television arrives

In the 1950s, the movie industry worried that moviegoers would stay at home watching black-and-white television instead of going to the movies. They lured audiences back by making films in color, like *Funny Face*. However, innovative black-and-white films still had the power to excite viewers.

New rules

The 1960s were full of new ideas for the film industry. French "New Wave" director Jean-Luc Godard rejected all the old rules of filmmaking and invented new ones. In Senegal, Ousmane Sembène paved the way for African filmmakers to tell their own stories, breaking away from the stereotyped African characters in US and European movies.

International blockbusters

By the early 1970s, martial arts films from East Asia had made international stars of Bruce Lee and Jackie Chan. The release of Spielberg's *Jaws* in 1975 created the first-ever summer blockbuster, inspiring a generation of imitators in Hollywood. In Bollywood, "masala" films mixed musical numbers, action, and comedy.

Animated experiences

In the 1980s, audiences flocked to see blockbuster action films at newly opened "megaplex" movie theaters with dozens of screens. Studio Ghibli's animation *Grave of the Fireflies* (1988) helped build the reputation of anime films outside their native Japan—the movie tells the story of a boy who looks after his little sister during World War II.

Grave of the Fireflies (1988).

Going digital

Blockbusters went from strength to strength in the 1990s, with the rise of special effects and computer animation. The first wholly computer-generated film was *Toy Story*, in 1995. Outside of Hollywood, US filmmakers took advantage of cheaper filmmaking equipment to make independent movies away from the big studios.

The rise of documentaries

Before the 2000s, no one thought audiences would get excited about documentaries at movie theaters, but the nature film *March of the Penguins* (2005, right) changed that. Digital technology also made it easier for ordinary people to make movies, resulting in *Super Size Me* (2004), another hit documentary—this time about eating too much fast food.

New technology

Demand for exciting new movies has held up well in the face of the internet. Spectacular 3-D films, such as the German dance film *Pina* (2011), have played a big part in engaging audiences, as have sequels to other successful films—for example, *Madagascar 3* made more money than either of the other *Madagascar* movies before it.

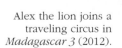

Alex the lion joins a traveling circus in *Madagascar 3* (2012).

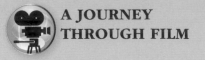
Pictures and movement

Photography

Early photography captured an image on a sheet of paper or metal. In the UK in the 1790s, Thomas Wedgewood experimented with heat and light to create pictures, but the first commercially successful process was unveiled in France by Louis-Jacques-Mandé Daguerre in 1839.

A 19th-century Daguerreotype camera

Optical toys

When we watch a movie, the continuous action we see is only an illusion of movement—individual images are shown one after the other so fast that they seem to be moving. In the 19th century, this illusion was used to create toys, such as the Praxinoscope shown below, which let viewers watch figures appear to move against different backgrounds.

Moving pictures

The **wonder of movies** is that even though they are based on technology that is hundreds of years old, they still seem like magic. It is hard to imagine what it must have been like for people to see their portrait in a photograph for the first time, or to watch the photographs come to life in moving pictures.

Ancient discovery

First used in the 16th century, the camera obscura (Latin for "dark room") was used as a toy or an artist's tool. When light from outside passes through a small hole in a dark box or room, it re-creates the outside image inside. The picture is clearer if a glass lens is added to the hole.

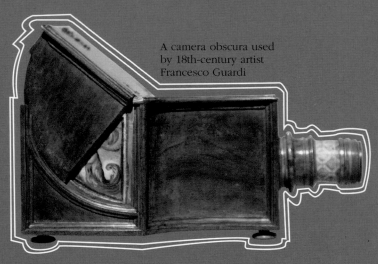

A camera obscura used by 18th-century artist Francesco Guardi

A man leaps over a high jump in this 1892 chronophotographic picture by Étienne-Jules Marey.

Chronophotography

The first images of movement were not meant for art or entertainment, but for science. In 1882, doctor and engineer Étienne-Jules Marey invented a "chronophotographic gun," which recorded a sequence of images to study movement. This led to the invention of moving pictures.

Five frames of an early film strip show an action sequence, with perforated sides to move the film through the projector.

The Kinetograph

Thomas Edison, inventor of the lightbulb, first came up with the idea for the Kinetograph camera in 1888. This camera took photographs very quickly, one after another on a strip of film. People watched the film in a special Kinetoscope machine—it whizzed the film strip past a light at 40 frames per second, creating the illusion of movement.

A train moves toward the camera in *The Arrival of a Train at La Ciotat Station* (1895).

The Cinematograph

Auguste and Louis Lumière developed the Cinematograph, a combined camera and projector. Their first public screening of a movie projected onto a screen in a dark room was in Paris in 1895. Audiences were amazed, and some panicked: When they saw the image of a train arriving at a station, some thought it was real and ran away.

A space rocket lands on the eye of the man in the Moon in *A Trip to the Moon*.

Who invented the movies?

Many different techniques were invented around the same time, so it is hard to say exactly who invented films. British director James Williamson was one of the first people to use a sequence of different shots edited together, in his dramatic rescue tale *Fire!* (1901). French director George Méliès used pioneering special effects to create aliens and a journey through space in the first-ever science-fiction movie, *A Trip to the Moon* (1902, shown right).

13

From silence to sound

For the first 32 years of moviemaking, there was no technology that recorded sound at the same time as moving images. Instead, filmmakers developed ways of telling **stories that did not rely on talking**. Actors used expressions and gestures to display emotions, and words would appear on screen to help explain the plot. When sound came along in 1927, the movies changed forever.

Rudolph Valentino stars in the 1926 film *The Son of the Sheik.*

From novelty act to big business

The first-ever silent films appeared at variety shows or fairgrounds as novelties. From 1905, permanent movie theaters began to open, and by the mid-1920s moviemaking was a multimillion dollar industry. Films were shown all over the world, making their stars internationally famous.

Silent stars

Actors in the silent era needed expressive faces and gestures to convey emotion without talking. Two actors who became stars thanks to their silent acting skills were American Clara Bow and Denmark's Asta Nielsen. In *It* (1927), Bow plays a spunky store clerk at a department store who is in love with her rich employer. Bow's irresistible charm—the "it factor"—makes him fall in love with her, too.

Clara Bow rose to stardom with silent films such as *It*.

The sound of silence

Silent films were not, in fact, completely silent. If you went to the movies before 1929 it would likely have been a very noisy experience. The action on screen was accompanied by music from a piano, and in bigger theaters there might even have been a full orchestra. In Brazil, singers performed behind the screen, and in Japan a live narrator, called a *benshi*, told the story of the film, speaking in different voices for each character.

Silent stories

Certain kinds of story were particularly well suited to silent film, such as horror films and slapstick comedies. Slapstick features people running into things and falling over—you do not need dialogue to get laughs if you can fall over in a funny way. *Why Worry?* (1923) features Harold Lloyd playing a man who is worried about his health.

Harold Lloyd makes friends with a giant man in *Why Worry?*

How was sound recorded?

The first film to feature synchronized sound and images was *The Jazz Singer* (1927). The sound was recorded on a separate disk from the film and then played at the same time as the image was projected. Technology quickly improved, and studios were soon able to record sound through the camera and onto the film itself.

An early sound projector

Helena Costello with her chorus girls in *Lights of New York* (1928)

The talkies arrive

The first all-talking feature film was *Lights of New York*. It became a massive hit, and now studios were able to create all-singing, all-dancing movies called musicals. Although these new films were exciting, their advent made the jobs of movie theater musicians obsolete. "Talkies" also ended the careers of silent stars who had poor speaking voices.

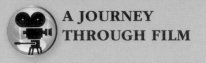

Biography

1889: Born in Walworth, London, UK. His parents were also entertainers.

1894: Makes his stage debut at age five, as a stand-in for his sick mother.

1910: Leaves for a tour of the US, with the comedy Karno Troupe.

1913: While performing in New York City, he is spotted by the Keystone Film Company and moves to California.

1914: Acts in his first film, *Making A Living,* and debuts as "The Tramp" in *Kid Auto Races at Venice.*

1919: Founds the United Artists Studio with three fellow performers.

1921: Directs his first feature length film, *The Kid.*

1931: His silent film *City Lights* is a great success, despite the introduction of sound to movies.

1940: Releases his first sound film, *The Great Dictator.*

Later years
In the 1940s, Chaplin began making movies in which he played a bad guy, such as the murderous husband in the comedy *Monsieur Verdoux* (1947). In 1952, he moved to Switzerland, and his final films were made in Europe.

Chaplin in *Monsieur Verdoux*

Charlie **Chaplin**

"A day without laughter is a day wasted."

Charlie Chaplin was a star of the silent era. Raised in a poor home in London, he grew up to become one of the **most recognizable faces in movie history**. A multitalented performer, director, and businessman, he cofounded a film studio, starred in more than 80 movies, and directed 11 feature films. Many of his films are still enjoyed by audiences today.

The Tramp

Chaplin's most famous character was "the Tramp," known for his baggy pants, shabby bowler hat, and toothbrush moustache. At a time when many people had very little money, the Tramp's optimism in the face of poverty made him popular around the world. In the 1921 film *The Kid*, the Tramp adopts a child and commits petty crimes with him.

Chaplin with child actor Jackie Coogan in *The Kid*

The perfectionist

In 1919, Chaplin cofounded the United Artists studio, which gave him the freedom to make his own creative decisions. He gained a reputation for perfectionism—he liked to do several "takes" of each shot, to make sure everything in them was exactly right.

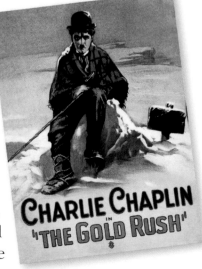

A poster for *The Gold Rush* (1925)

Tears of a clown

Chaplin started his career mainly playing the clown, but he soon decided he wanted to make films that were moving as well as funny. *City Lights* (1931, left) is a great example of this. It shows the Tramp falling in love with a blind flower girl, and it contains many laugh-out-loud moments, but with a final scene that is sure to bring a tear to your eye.

Still silent

Even after "talkies" were introduced in the late 1920s, Chaplin continued making silent films, partly because he feared the Tramp character would lose his international appeal if he spoke in one particular language. Chaplin made some of his best silent movies in the sound era, including *Modern Times* (1936, below).

Chaplin plays the role of a factory worker in *Modern Times*.

Jacques Tati as Monsieur Hulot, a character in *Mon Oncle* (1958) that was inspired by Charlie Chaplin

Chaplin's legacy

In addition to entertaining generations of comedy fans, Chaplin was the inspiration for several cartoon characters, including Mickey Mouse, and he influenced silent comics such as Britain's Mr. Bean and French comic Jacques Tati (see pages 128–129). Tati said: "Without [Chaplin], I would never have made a film." In 1999, *Time* magazine included Charlie Chaplin alongside world leaders in its list of the 100 most influential people of the 20th century.

Stranger *than fiction*

The earliest films recorded real life, since it was easy to capture but still interesting for audiences who had not seen movies before. Filmmakers, however, kept looking for new ways to entertain, and they soon discovered how to edit images together to **create dramatic stories**, ushering in an exciting period of discovery in filmmaking.

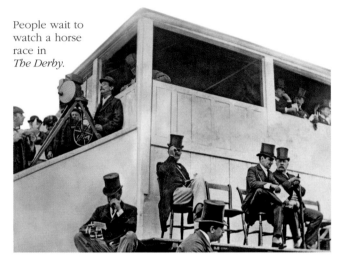

People wait to watch a horse race in *The Derby*.

Actuality films

An early form of documentary, actuality films were records of real events. Like taking a photograph, the films were made by placing a camera in one position to capture the action in front of it. The Lumière brothers introduced this form of documentary, filming workers leaving a factory. In 1895, the technique was used to catch the exciting finish of a horse race in *The Derby*.

Newsreel

Early news reports, called newsreels, were made up of silent documentary films about topical events and current affairs. Invented by the Pathé brothers, they were initially shown in newsreel theaters, but later screened before feature films.

A poster advertising Pathé Brothers

Poetic license

The truth does not have to be boring. Although Russian director Dziga Vertov did not like fiction filmmaking, he experimented with inventive storytelling techniques in his documentaries. *Man with a Movie Camera* (1929) takes us on a whirlwind ride through Odessa, Ukraine, with freeze frames, slow-motion, and jump-cuts between scenes.

An eye appears within a camera lens in *Man with a Movie Camera*.

A silent film, *October* (1928) recounts the 1917 Russian Revolution in the style of a documentary.

Propaganda

Propaganda films promote one side of an argument in an attempt to persuade the audience to agree. *October* is a dramatic account of the Russian Revolution in October 1917. It was commissioned by the Soviet government to celebrate the 10th anniversary of its rise to power and to convince Soviet citizens of how good their leadership was.

Neorealism

With their film studios destroyed and their nation impoverished after World War II, Italian directors broke away from tradition and began filming on the streets. A style called "neorealism," which focused on the everyday issues of the working classes, was born. *La Terra Trema* (1948) used nonprofessional actors to tell the story of a small fishing village struggling to make money.

The cast of *La Terra Trema* was made up of local people from Aci Trezza in Sicily.

Storytelling tricks

Battleship Potemkin (1925)

This film, by director Sergei Eisenstein, is one of the most famous examples of propaganda. A fictional account of the rebellious crew of a warship, the *Potemkin*, the film's "Odessa Steps" sequence—where citizens are chased by soldiers—is known for its editing and early use of montage.

Montage Montage is the editing together of quick shots of the same scene to build tension. First, Eisenstein focuses on the terror in a mother's face as she sees her son falling.

Building tension The film cuts between images of the soldiers walking down the steps shooting and the mother picking up her son amid the chaos.

Wide shot The camera pulls out to show a wider picture of the mother walking up toward the soldiers, screaming at them to stop shooting.

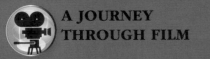

Before there were movie theaters...

Bioscope

Before the first permanent movie theaters were built, "Bioscopes" were popular attractions at Music Halls and traveling fairs. Viewers could watch a variety of short films, accompanied by music. The movies were mostly simple stories, but that did not matter— audiences loved the novelty of moving pictures and demanded more.

Mutoscope

Some of the earliest films were shown on "viewing machines" such as the Kinetoscope and Mutoscope (both invented in 1894). These devices allowed one person at a time to watch a short film by putting a coin into the slot, looking into the viewing lens, and turning a crank handle. The machines are still popular in many countries today.

A Mutoscope from the early 20th century

Going to the movies

The art of moviemaking has changed a lot since moving images were first recorded in the late 19th century, and so has the **experience of watching a movie**. The traditional theater with rows of seats and a big screen has been joined by drive-ins, 3-D films, and even cell phones.

The great escape

In the 1920s, movie theaters were known as "dream houses," places where people could escape from the real world into the fantasy world of movies. With their elaborate architecture, exotic decoration, and well-dressed, uniformed attendants, theaters created a magical atmosphere that was as important to audiences as the movies themselves.

Drive-in theaters let you enjoy your movie in the great outdoors.

At the drive-in

These days, most movie theaters are "multiplexes"—large theaters with several screens. But there are still plenty of more unusual places to see a film. In countries with good weather, outdoor screenings are popular, such as "drive-ins," where you park your car in front of the screen. Some cities have outdoor theaters on rooftops. One unusual theater is the Sol Cinema in Wales; it is a mobile theater in an adapted truck, powered entirely by solar energy.

This 1920s theater in San Francisco is typical of the bright lights and colorful decoration of traditional movie theaters.

Moviegoing madness

In the 1950s and 1960s, director William Castle used fun gimmicks to make his horror movies more scary. He arranged for a glow-in-the-dark skeleton to float through the movie theater at showings of *House on Haunted Hill* (1959) and hid buzzing motors under seats to surprise viewers at *The Tingler* (1959). Audiences today are more likely to be drawn in by three-dimensional (3-D) effects.

3-D films wow audiences by making it seem as though objects are zooming out of the screen right into the theater.

Watching movies on your phone

You used to have to go to the movies to see the latest film. Now, thanks to new technology, you can see a movie whenever and wherever you like. Direct streaming services let you watch movies on demand, while online services allow you to download films to a computer to view at home. You can even watch movies on your cell phone, so you can enjoy them any time. Some people think that watching movies this way means we miss out on the best parts of moviegoing—laughing, gasping, and crying with a room of other film fans.

Heroes *and* villains

As films became popular and widespread, certain types of **audience-pleasing characters** began to appear again and again, forming an instantly recognizable cast of heroes and villains. Tough guys muscle in on action and gangster films, swashbuckling adventurers swoop in and save the day, and an ordinary person in an extraordinary situation can become a hero, too.

◀ ***Dracula* (1931)** Horror villains can be terrifying, from evil serial killers to flesh-eating zombies. In *Dracula*, Bela Lugosi plays the ultimate horror villain Count Dracula. The people he meets find him charming, right up to the moment when he tries to suck their blood. Dracula's long black cape and hypnotic powers create a sense of drama, so even his most horrible deeds are pretty stylish.

▶ ***The Public Enemy* (1931)** One of Hollywood's most popular characters is the classic tough guy—he is brooding, unpredictable, and often violent. James Cagney portrays this perfectly in *The Public Enemy*, playing the role of gangster Tom Powers. Cagney's acting skills let Tom's heart of gold shine through, even when he is behaving badly.

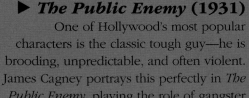

Actor Errol Flynn as the legendary hero Robin Hood in *The Adventures of Robin Hood*

▼ *The Adventures of Robin Hood* **(1938)** The swashbuckling hero always nabs the bad guy and saves the damsel in distress. A classic example in this adventure film is dashing Robin Hood, a man who steals from the rich to give to the poor. Robin, along with his outlaw army, defends the English people against the bully Prince John. Not only is Robin brave enough to take on several sword-fighting opponents at once, but he also always has a clever quip, ready to deliver at the perfect moment.

◄ *The Glass Key* **(1942)**
The *femme fatale*—French for "deadly woman"—has irresistible charm but can be dangerous. This type of character is often associated with film noir—movies that feature dark deeds. For instance, in *The Glass Key,* when two men fall in love with the beautiful Janet (played by Veronica Lake) the complications include political corruption, beatings, and murder. The *femme fatale* isn't all bad, though— by the end of a movie she is usually sorry for causing trouble.

► *Doctor Zhivago* **(1965)** Set over several
decades in Russian history, this movie tells the story of Lara and Doctor Zhivago, who fall in love despite many obstacles. Like romantic heroes in other films, Zhivago is handsome, kind, and a little mysterious. So while Lara is falling in love with him, some of the audience might be, too.

◄ *It's a Wonderful Life* **(1946)** The everyman
is a character that audiences can easily relate to—he is an ordinary man who, in extraordinary situations, rises to be a hero. In *It's a Wonderful Life*, James Stewart plays George Bailey, who helps many people in his town, but wonders if it was all worthwhile when things get tough. George is not especially brave or clever, but he is so likeable that you can't help rooting for him.

► *La Belle et la Bête* **(1946)** Unlike
the damsel in distress who waits to be rescued, the quiet-but-resourceful heroine relies on her own wits. Belle (played by Josette Day) tries to save her father from the beast in *La Belle et la Bête*, showing strong qualities like patience and bravery.

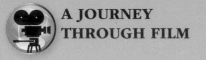

Biography

1901: Born in Chicago.

1917: Leaves school and joins the Red Cross.

1919: Begins his artistic career as a newspaper cartoonist.

1922: Founds Laugh-O-Gram, making short animated films, but ends up in debt and has to close.

1923: Sets up The Disney Brothers Studio with his brother Roy.

1928: Creates *Steamboat Willie*, the first Mickey Mouse cartoon with sound.

1929: Invents *Silly Symphonies*, a series of short cartoons that were based on musical themes rather than a continuing cast of characters.

1937: Premieres *Snow White and the Seven Dwarfs*.

1940: Produces *Fantasia*, featuring animated characters in sequences set to classical music.

1966: Dies, age 65.

Awards

Walt Disney received 66 Academy Award nominations and won 32 Oscars—both are world records. His final Oscar, for *Winnie the Pooh and the Blustery Day*, was awarded three years after his death. Asteroid 4017 Disneya, discovered in 1980, was named in his honor.

Walt Disney

"When people laugh at Mickey Mouse, it's because he's so human; and that is the secret of his popularity."

An artist and a showman, Walt Disney is the most **famous animator** of all time. He was the first person to add sound to a cartoon, he invented **feature-length animated films**, and he was awarded 26 Oscars in his lifetime.

Mickey Mouse in *Steamboat Willie*

Breaking ground

After a number of earlier animation attempts, Disney hit the big time in 1928 with *Steamboat Willie*. It introduced Mickey Mouse and was the first cartoon with synchronized sound instead of just music.

Feature films

In 1937, Disney made *Snow White and the Seven Dwarfs*, the first-ever feature-length animated film with sound. It took three years to make and cost more than double what had been expected. It was a box-office hit, and Disney was given an honorary Oscar—one big statue and seven little ones. He went on to make many other successful feature-length animations, including *Bambi* (1942), about a young deer growing up without its mother.

Beyond animation

Disney didn't just make animated films—he also made live-action feature films, such as *Treasure Island* (1950), and films that were a mixture of the two, like *Mary Poppins* (1964). *Mary Poppins* includes scenes where human actors appear alongside animated characters. It was nominated for 13 Oscars and won six.

Julie Andrews as the magical nanny Mary Poppins

Disneyland

Walt Disney dreamed of an amazing place where children and their parents could enjoy themselves together. In 1955, he realized this dream, opening the giant theme park Disneyland in California. It cost him $17 million to create and contained rides in five different themed "lands." In addition to the original California resort, there are now Disney theme parks in Florida, Paris, Tokyo, Hong Kong, and Shanghai.

Cinderella Castle in Walt Disney World, Florida

Monsters, Inc. (2001), is a Disney Pixar film about a city of monsters who create power for their city by scaring children.

Snow White wakes up and meets the Seven Dwarfs, who try to keep her hidden from her stepmother—an evil Queen.

Disney after Walt

After Disney died in 1966, his company continued to flourish. It now owns several other film studios, including Pixar (maker of *Toy Story* and *Monsters, Inc.*) and Lucasfilm (maker of *Star Wars*). The Walt Disney Company's own studio continues to produce blockbuster films, such as the *Pirates of the Caribbean* series.

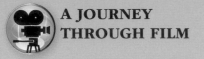
Technicolor timeline

1906 George Albert Smith invents "Kinemacolor" in the UK—he projects black-and-white film through red and green filters.

1914 The world's first color feature-film is made. It is a movie about mistaken identity called *The World, the Flesh and the Devil*.

1922 *The Toll of The Sea* is the first color feature-film shot in Hollywood. Most scenes are shot outside to make sure there is enough light.

1934 The first three-color camera is invented, and blue appears on screen for the first time.

1937 Disney has a big hit with its first full-color animated feature, *Snow White and the Seven Dwarfs*.

1939 MGM releases *The Wizard of Oz*. It features a few black-and-white scenes, then bursts into color.

1949 Kodak develops Eastmancolor film—a process that is easier than Technicolor, but creates less vibrant colors.

1954 Color is used to win audiences away from black-and-white television. By the mid-1950s, about half of all movies are in color.

Technicolor camera

Glorious Technicolor

Techniques to color black-and-white film have existed almost since the beginning of moviemaking, but none really took off until the **Technicolor process** was developed. Some filmmakers disliked this new look, believing that movies that were too similar to real life couldn't be art. Movie fans, however, rushed to movie theaters, and color was a big hit.

The Phantom of the Opera was filmed using the two-color system—scenes are seen in red and green.

Early color

If you watch the color scene from *The Phantom of the Opera* (1925), you might notice the lack of blue. This was a major problem of the early two-color system—the limited red-green spectrum it used made blue impossible to reproduce. For this reason, any sky or sea always had a strong green tinge.

Color before Technicolor

Filmmakers tried all kinds of methods to inject color into their movies before Technicolor came along. Early innovators would project black-and-white film through colored filters or painstakingly hand-paint every frame with color. To bathe a whole scene in the same color, dyes were used. Different colors had different meanings—for instance, blue meant that a scene was set at night.

Three-color Technicolor

Fully colored movies were created by passing three strips of film through a camera at the same time. The process required big cameras and very bright lights to work properly. These lights heated the sets to very high temperatures, which made Technicolor shoots an uncomfortable experience for the actors involved.

Technicolor triumphs

Some genres, like shady film noir, seemed so suited to black-and-white that trying them in color was a risky experiment. In *Leave Her To Heaven* (1945), however, the showy outfits of leading lady Ellen look appropriately garish, and the blue lake where she commits a murder looks alarmingly deep.

A poster for *Leave Her To Heaven*

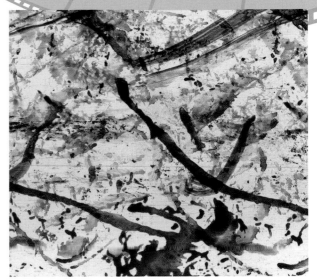

Begone Dull Care (1949) uses color to reflect jazz music.

Color in animation

Disney's *Flowers and Trees*, released in 1932, was the first animation to use the three-color Technicolor system. Full-color was popular for animations, and by the 1940s, experimental animators like Norman McLaren had made color a key feature of their films. *Begone Dull Care* uses moving color to replicate the sound of jazz music visually.

Scarlett O'Hara and Rhett Butler gaze into each others eyes in *Gone With the Wind* (1939), which was filmed in three-color Technicolor.

Black-and-white film is used to suggest the past in *Pleasantville*.

Brilliant black-and-white

Modern movies are still sometimes shot in black-and-white. This could be to re-create the feel of the past, or simply because the director likes the way it looks. The 1998 movie *Pleasantville* begins in color, but becomes black-and-white when the characters are sucked into a 1950s sitcom through their TV set.

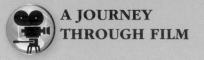
In the beginning...

What came before

There had already been earlier film adaptations of Frank L. Baum's book *The Wonderful Wizard of Oz* before the 1939 version. In 1925, Larry Semon directed and starred in a silent black-and-white film, playing a farmhand who must help Dorothy, a long-lost princess, return to the land of Oz.

The Wizard of Oz (1925), starring Dorothy Dwan and Larry Semon

Troubled shoot

The 1939 film was beset by problems while shooting. The actor playing the Tin Man reacted badly to his makeup and had to be hospitalized, as was the Wicked Witch, who was badly burned by a special effect. Added to this was the Technicolor lighting that made the sets very hot.

Special effects

The dazzling special effects of this film were the best ever seen at the time. Most famously, the movie starts in black-and-white, but then turns Technicolor, and in the scene where Dorothy pours water on the Wicked Witch of the West, a platform built into the floor sinks, giving the impression that the Witch is melting.

If Dorothy taps the heels of her ruby slippers together three times they will take her home to Kansas.

The Wizard of Oz

This movie has enchanted generations of children since it was made, nearly 75 years ago. Starring Judy Garland as Dorothy, a little girl who is transported to a **magical land called Oz**, it includes memorable songs, lovable characters, and a pair of magic ruby slippers.

The story goes… Dorothy finds life dull on a farm in Kansas with her Aunt and Uncle. Worse still, a neighbor threatens to destroy her dog, Toto. However, everything changes when a tornado sweeps the farmhouse off into the sky, with Dorothy and Toto inside. Dorothy wakes to find herself in a magical, multicolored land called Oz. Along with a tin man, a scarecrow, and a cowardly lion, Dorothy sets off on a journey to the Emerald City to try and find a wizard who will grant them all their greatest wishes. But why do her new friends look so familiar? And what if the Wicked Witch of the West catches them first?

Glinda the Good Witch rescues Dorothy from the Wicked Witch of the West.

The Wicked Witch

The green-skinned Wicked Witch of the West is one of the most memorable movie villains of all time. She blames Dorothy for the death of her sister, the Wicked Witch of the East, who is accidentally crushed by Dorothy's house when it lands in Oz. The Wicked Witch uses her flying monkey army to seek revenge.

The Wizard

The Wizard of Oz is much feared and respected throughout the land that bears his name, although few people have ever met him. Dorothy believes that if anyone can help her get back home to Kansas, he can. When she finally meets him, however, she soon begins to suspect that the "Great and Powerful Oz" might not be all that he pretends to be.

The Wizard of Oz appears as a frightening green floating head.

Judy Garland as Dorothy, with the Tin Man, Scarecrow, and the Cowardly Lion

Farther along the yellow brick road

What came after

With its magical plot and universal message of hope and friendship, it is no surprise that *The Wizard of Oz* is such a popular story. The 1939 film is frequently shown on television, it has has inspired several stage shows, and songs from the movie, including "Somewhere Over The Rainbow," have been rerecorded by pop singers.

***The Wiz* (1978)** This film transposed the story of Oz into modern-day Harlem, New York. Dorothy is a schoolteacher who has never been far from home—until she gets caught in a whirlwind and transported to Oz.

Wicked This Broadway musical stars a green-skinned and fiery-tempered girl named Elphaba, who grows up to become the Wicked Witch of the West. Elphaba has a falling out with her popular and beautiful childhood friend, Glinda, who becomes the Good Witch of the North.

The Golden Age of the movies

From the end of the silent movies in the late 1920s to the beginning of the 60s, movies poured nonstop out of the studios and **audiences packed movie theaters** as never before or since. These years are called the "Golden Age" of the movies, when film technology kept getting better, and the thrills and glamorous stars of the big screen swept audiences into new worlds.

The gate at Paramount Studios, Hollywood, 1927

The big studios

Mega-sized movie studios such as MGM in the United States and Pathé in France were known as "filmmaking factories." These giant companies managed absolutely everything about a movie's production, the movie theaters, and the actors. The tycoons in charge had total power, even over the lifestyles of their top stars.

Seeing stars

MGM once declared that it owned "more stars than there are in heaven." In the Golden Age, many actors shot to fame overnight. Their huge fees paid for the Hollywood lifestyles that were the dream of every young movie fan, and a starstruck public loved seeing and reading about them.

Two of the biggest Hollywood names of the era: Rock Hudson and Elizabeth Taylor in *Giant* (1956)

European movies

The Golden Age wasn't limited to Hollywood. Germany's main movie studio, Universum Film AG (UFA), grew big in the 1920s. It invested in sound equipment and made the transition to talkies when other companies didn't. Some European filmmakers copied Hollywood; others either didn't want to or couldn't afford to. Italian filmmakers in the 1940s and 50s moved away from the Hollywood style, creating a new form of "real life" filmmaking called "Neo (new) realism."

Miracle in Milan (1951) was filmed on the streets. It featured local people as well as professional actors.

Tales from Tokyo

The 1950s were the start of a great period for Japanese cinema. A new kind of storytelling was invented with *Rashomon* (1950), which tells the tale of a serious crime from several different viewpoints. *Godzilla* (1954), starring a giant mutant lizard, spawned several other monster movies, and the family drama *Tokyo Story* (1953) is often voted the best movie ever made.

Different characters tell a different version of the same tale in *Rashomon*. But which one is true?

Did TV kill the movies?

What brought the movie's Golden Age to an end? Partly, it was the arrival of the small screen. From the 1950s onward, more and more people bought TVs and stayed in at night rather than going out to the movies. Also, it became harder to make money on movies and very easy to lose it. Production costs kept rising and no one could afford to take the risk of making a film that might flop. The bigger studios gradually became less powerful and produced fewer movies each year.

Classic films

Once seen, never forgotten

A classic is best described as a movie that goes on pleasing audiences decades after it was first made. Some films make a big splash for a few weeks and are then never heard of again, but a classic is loved from one generation to the next.

Swiss Miss (1938): a typical Laurel and Hardy farce.

The 1930s Comedy duo Laurel and Hardy, silent stars who were also a hit in the talkies, made many movies that still cause helpless laughter.

Casablanca (1942): a war story and a love story rolled into one

The 1940s A nail-biting plot, plus fine acting from Ingrid Bergman and Humphrey Bogart, make *Casablanca* one of the all-time movie greats.

The 1950s Following India's struggle for independence, *Mother India* helped to build the country's national identity. This is an epic melodrama of heroism in the face of poverty and injustice.

Mother India (1957): a tale of survival

31

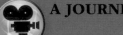

Stars of the Golden Age

Movie stars are more than just successful actors—they are also the difference between a blockbuster hit and a flop, because loyal fans will often see a movie just because their favorite star is in it. The way stars talk, look, and behave depends a lot on the age in which they lived: the actors of Hollywood's Golden Age cultivated glamorous, larger-than-life personas that still captivate audiences today.

Clark Gable plays suave Rhett Butler in *Gone with the Wind* (1939).

▲ **Clark Gable** A smooth dress sense and a gruff manner are qualities Gable shared with his famous onscreen character Rhett Butler, from *Gone with the Wind*. A typical romantic lead, Gable did his best work opposite his favorite leading ladies, including Joan Crawford, Jean Harlow, and Myrna Loy. He had a carrot-eating scene in *It Happened One Night* (1934) that became the inspiration for the Bugs Bunny cartoons.

▶ **Marlene Dietrich**

This German actress and singer began her screen career playing small parts in the silent films of the 1920s. She leapt to fame in 1930, becoming a superstar after performing in her first talkie, *Blue Angel*, about the relationship between a dancer and a schoolteacher. Dietrich became a US citizen in 1939 and entertained US troops on the frontlines throughout World War II.

Marlene Dietrich plays a beautiful dancer in *Blue Angel*.

▼ **Carmen Miranda** The "Brazilian Bombshell" brought a hint of the exotic to 1940s America, with the help of Samba music and a memorable fruit-covered hat. She was criticized in Brazil for promoting a Latin-American stereotype, but, by 1945, films such as *That Night in Rio* (1941) and *The Gang's All Here* (1943) had made her the highest paid actress in the US.

Carmen Miranda in *Copacabana* (1947)

◀ **Humphrey Bogart**
This leading actor started out playing tough guys, but by the time he was in *Casablanca* (1942) he had established the screen persona for which he is remembered— a world-weary, street-smart cynic. This was a good fit for the hard-boiled detectives Bogart played in movies like *The Maltese Falcon* (1941) and *The Big Sleep* (1946).

Humphrey Bogart in *Casablanca*

◀ **Marilyn Monroe**
This screen legend is usually remembered for her looks, but she was a natural at comedy, and she took lessons to improve her acting skills. On screen she often played the role of a gold-digging beauty in musicals such as *Gentlemen Prefer Blondes* (1953)—shown left—and *How To Marry A Millionaire* (1953).

◀ **James Dean** Dean remains one of Hollywood's most recognizable faces. This is especially outstanding, since he acted in only three feature films before his death in a car crash, at the age of just 24. His raw performance in *Rebel Without a Cause* (1955) was a revelation for audiences more used to a formal, theatrical style, and it made him particularly popular with teenagers.

A promotional poster for *Rebel Without a Cause*, starring James Dean

Sidney Poitier as a teacher with his class in *To Sir, With Love* (1967)

▲ **Sidney Poitier** The Civil Rights era in the late 1950s and 1960s was a time of inspiring change, and the actor who best represented that period was Poitier. A living, breathing rejection of racism in *To Sir, With Love* and *In the Heat of the Night* (1967), he radiates intelligence and integrity. He went on to direct a number of popular movies, such as *Uptown Saturday Night* (1974) and *Let's Do It Again* (1975).

▲ **Elizabeth Taylor**
From her performance in *National Velvet* (1944), Taylor went on to become one of Hollywood's most iconic stars. She is almost as well-known for her eight marriages and flamboyant jewelry collection as she is for her roles in classic films such as *Cat on a Hot Tin Roof* (1958) and *Cleopatra* (1963), above.

The studio system

In many ways, the Golden Age of Hollywood was a factory for the production of movie stars, where actors were contracted to work for a single movie studio. The raw material—an attractive, anonymous teenager—was transformed with a new name, a new wardrobe, acting lessons, and voice coaching. Actors' contracts with the studio often included a "morality clause," which told them how to behave, both in public and in private.

Moving to the modern age

Since the end of Hollywood's Golden Age in the 1960s, **exciting new film industries have sprung up all over the world.** This is partly because digital technology has made moviemaking accessible to people who could never have afforded to make a film before. For movie fans this can only be good news—it means a host of new stories and new voices.

Alice and Philip take a train ride in *Alice in the Cities*.

European influence

"New Wave" cinema in France in the 1960s moved away from traditional styles, using new filmmaking and editing techniques to tell stories. The movement heavily influenced European moviemaking, as seen in films such as *Alice in the Cities* (1974). This German film has long scenes with no dialogue.

In *Waiting for Happiness*, Abdallah tries to absorb the culture of his mother's village.

Booming Africa

Films have been made in Africa since the 1960s, but it was the affordability of video technology in the 1990s that transformed the Nigerian film industry into "Nollywood," the world's second largest film industry after Mumbai's Bollywood. Nigeria is not the only country in Africa to tap this potential. *Waiting for Happiness* (2002) was made in the West African nation of Mauritania. It is about a 17-year-old boy named Abdallah who visits his mother's seaside village.

Valentin from Argentina became a huge international hit.

Latin American mix

Many modern Latin American filmmakers from Argentina, Brazil, and Mexico are influenced by the "Third Cinema" movement of the 1960s and 70s. This rejected Hollywood's commercial style of making movies, and portrayed people's struggles and aspirations in a way that struck a chord with audiences. For instance, the Argentinian film *Valentin* (2002) tells the story of an 8-year-old boy, Noya, who tries to deal with life's obstacles by meddling in the lives of grown-ups.

Magical Bollywood

Mumbai's Hindi-speaking Bollywood movie industry is one of the oldest in the world, but it still moves with the times. Newer Bollywood films no longer rely solely on melodrama, but instead focus on innovative storylines and use cutting-edge technologies and special effects—as seen in the superhero science-fiction film *Ra.One* (2011).

A song from *Ra.One*, featuring Kareena Kapoor

American independents

The word "independent" or "indie" is used to describe American movies that are made outside the traditional Hollywood system. These films have smaller budgets, but this means that there is less pressure to make money with ticket sales. This gives indie filmmakers the freedom to explore offbeat characters, such as the lead in *Napoleon Dynamite* (2004), a bullied high school kid with unusual hobbies, such as practicing ninja moves and drawing fantasy creatures.

Napoleon Dynamite stars Jon Heder (center) in the geeky title role.

Children's movies

Most movies look at the world from an adult's point of view, but some films are designed to deal with things that are important to children, such as school, making friends, and relationships with parents. With such universal themes, all countries make movies for children, but some make more than others. Many children's films are animated, but since the 1950s live action has become increasingly popular.

***The Goonies* (1985)** In this American action-adventure comedy, a bunch of kids get together to save their "Goon Docks" homes from demolition. In the process, they stumble upon an old map that leads to the long-lost treasure of the 17th-century pirate One-Eyed Willie.

***Une Vie de Chat* (2010)** Animated animals often pop up in children's films, but the cat in this French movie is more clever than cute—he smartly involves Parisian girl Zoé in a thrilling roof-top adventure. Released in English as *A Cat in Paris*, the movie was praised for its hand-drawn animation, which harkens back to older-style films.

Behind
the scenes

There is a lot more to movies than what we see on screen. Behind the actors and directors, **a whole team of specialists** are at work, creating props, costumes, sets, and special effects.

From green light *to* opening night

All movies go through similar **stages of production**, whether they are made by a crew of unpaid friends and family or put together by a huge established movie studio with a big budget. Here is how moviemakers go about their work, from thinking up the first idea to showing off the finished product.

The first spark

Every movie begins with an idea. This idea could come from a book that a director or scriptwriter loves, or start with a few lines scribbled on the back of a napkin, maybe inspired by a dinner conversation. Before the full script is written, this initial idea will be written up as a "treatment," which consists of a few pages describing the plot and tone of the film.

Screenwriting

Once the treatment is finished, it is time to start writing the screenplay—the movie script. One screenplay will usually have to be rewritten several times before the producers are completely happy. Different drafts will try out different endings or scene orders, and specialized writers are sometimes hired to work on particular aspects, such as the dialogue or action.

Marilyn Monroe signs her contract for *Some Like It Hot* (1959), watched by producer Walter Mirisch.

The pitch

Once they have a screenplay they are happy with, producers will present, or "pitch," a film to investors. The investors will decide whether to fund a movie based on the screenplay, how successful similar films have been, and the reputation of the director or actors involved. In industry slang, a movie that has enough money to get made has been given a "green light."

Preproduction

The producers allocate a budget to each department, and they plan the shoot down to the last detail. The hope is to avoid any costly mistakes later on in production. It is the job of the art department to create storyboard action sequences and plan the general "look" of the film.

Storyboard for *Gone with the Wind* (1939)

Cast and crew

Now is the time to cast smaller roles that were not filled at the pitch stage. A casting agent will negotiate with actors' agents to get the right person for every role, and each department must "crew up" its own department.

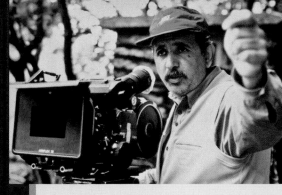

Iranian director Majid Majidi on set in 2001

On set

Finally, it is time for the cameras to roll. Depending on what is in the script, the actual shoot can take anything from a week to a year. Working days often last between 12 and 18 hours, but much of the activity that takes place is not performing the scenes, but preparing for them. Sets are constructed, lighting is assembled, and actors get dressed up in costumes and makeup.

Postproduction

At this stage all the different elements created during production are combined and edited into a finished film. This used to involve cutting celluloid film and reassembling scenes in the correct order. Now it is all done digitally, as is the addition of the soundtrack and any computer-generated special effects. A movie is "locked" when a director is happy and there are no more changes to be made.

Marketing and publicity

The distribution company is also responsible for attracting audiences to see the movie, by creating an eye-catching poster, a memorable trailer, and encouraging "word-of-mouth" marketing on sites like Facebook and Twitter. During the publicity stage, the stars of the movie travel the world to talk about it in press interviews. When several interviews take place on the same day, it is called a "media junket."

Movie posters for *Men in Black* (1997)

Distribution

Once a movie is made, a distribution company will buy the rights to it and decide how and when it will be seen by an audience. This used to be as simple as negotiating with movie theater owners and arranging for the film reels to be shipped to theaters around the world. Now, however, movies can be sent to theaters digitally and made available to audiences via DVD, television broadcast, and online download.

Premiere

This is the most glamorous part of the whole process, when all the cast gets dressed up to attend the film's very first public screening. Photographs of the stars' red carpet outfits appear in the press and help promote the movie, reminding people it will soon be released in theaters.

Bollywood actress Sonam Kapoor attends the 66th Cannes Film Festival in 2013.

The box office

Movie tickets used to be sold from a small booth or "box office." The term is still used to refer to all the money that a film makes. When a film does well at the box office, it becomes easier for movies that are similar to it to get made. If it does badly, the careers of everyone who was involved in making it can be damaged.

Who's *who*

Every shoot involves the work of **many different members of the film "crew,"** and on a big-budget production, this can run into thousands of people. If you watch a movie until the very end, you will see that the credits include mysterious job titles such as "best boy" and "runners"—but what do they all do?

Model of a ship animated in *The Pirates! In an Adventure with Scientists* (2012)

Art

The art department is responsible for the "look" of a movie. It is headed by a production designer or an art director, who oversees the work of a team of set decorators and storyboard artists. In preproduction, the art department works closely with the director to decide on the visual themes of the movie, for example, "futuristic" for a science-fiction film. The art department then creates sketches and models for the whole crew to work from.

Colleen Atwood, costume designer for *Snow White and the Huntsman* (2012), poses with a cloak she made out of rooster feathers. With the magic of special effects, it was transformed into a flock of crows.

Costume

The costume department makes sure all the actors are dressed in a way that suits their character and the period of the film. If they cannot rent or buy the right clothes, they design and tailor them from scratch. Once the film shooting begins, the wardrobe supervisor and costume assistants must dress the actors, keep track of the film's costumes, and repair or replace any damaged items.

Grips and gaffers

Grips are the technicians who set up the cameras on a movie set, sometimes on moving apparatus such as a dolly or crane. The gaffer is the chief of the electrical crew who, with the help of a deputy called the "best boy," sets up complex lighting rigs that can transform night into day, and vice versa.

This film crew is using dolly tracks and a remote-controlled crane at the Colosseum in Rome.

Camera team

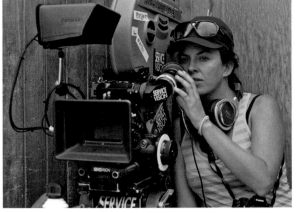

The head of the camera team is the director of photography (DoP), or cinematographer. The camera team also includes a camera operator, a "focus puller," who makes sure the image is clear, and a clapper loader, who operates the famous clapperboard at the beginning of each take.

Even the director must know how the film cameras work. Here, director Claudia Llosa checks out the equipment on set.

Postproduction

Once filming is complete, the editor shapes the visual and sound material into a finished movie, usually working with the director and helped by a team of assistant editors. The colorist adjusts the images so they are even throughout the film, and the visual effects team adds special effects.

Different parts of a movie are put together in postproduction.

More roles

2nd AD helps the 1st AD (assistant director) and ensures that the cast is ready for action.

Breakdown artists specialize in making new clothes appear old, ragged, and dirty.

Greensmen design landscapes by finding appropriate foliage or building fake plants.

Runners are often young people starting out in the industry; they run around to help other crew.

Unit publicist arranges for on-set photos and journalist visits to publicize the movie.

Weapons master is responsible for safely maintaining guns, knives, and any other weapons.

Casting director researches and secures stars for leading roles, as well as hundreds of "extras" for crowd scenes.

Location scout finds the best places to film and obtains permission to shoot there.

Dialect coach helps the actors perfect the accents of the characters they play.

Body double stands in for an actor in shots that involve skills the actor does not have or that may put him or her in danger.

Script supervisor keeps an eye on the script to ensure continuity between takes.

Boom operator makes sure microphones are in the right places to record sound.

Color grader alters and enhances the colors of a movie during postproduction.

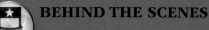

Great producers

Producers **organize a film from beginning to end**. Typically, they are responsible for choosing a good script and securing the rights to it, finding the money to pay for the movie, and settling any disagreements that might come up during the shoot. Great producers do not always get as much credit as great directors, but without them movies would never get made in the first place.

◀ **David O. Selznick** The very model of an ambitious movie mogul, Selznick worked behind the scenes in Hollywood from 1926 until the late 1950s, and he produced many classics. His towering achievement was *Gone with the Wind* (1939)—it held the record for the highest earning movie in history for over 25 years.

▼ **Kathleen Kennedy** The "Queen of the Hollywood blockbuster" can claim credit for films that have made over $11 million around the world. She has produced several of the most popular movies of all time, including *E.T. The Extra-Terrestrial* (1982) and *Jurassic Park* (1993). The regular working partner of director Steven Spielberg, Kennedy has also collaborated with *Back to the Future* (1985) director Robert Zemeckis and *Star Wars* director George Lucas.

Kathleen Kennedy with Steven Spielberg on the set of *Jurassic Park* (1993)

◀ **Eric Fellner** As co-owner of the UK's largest production company, Working Title Films, Fellner is responsible for many great successes. His productions are often set in Britain and have a distinctly British feel, such as *Johnny English* (2003) and *Nanny McPhee* (2005, shown left), which stars Emma Thompson as a Mary Poppins-style magical nanny to seven mischievous siblings.

▶ **Weinstein Bros.** Harvey and Bob Weinstein managed what no other producers had done before: presenting independently made and specialty art films to a mainstream audience. They have turned such as *The Iron Lady* (2011, shown right) into both multiple Oscar winners and box-office hits.

▲ **Yash Chopra** A major force in Bollywood, Yash "King of Romance" Chopra founded India's biggest production company, Yash Raj Films. He produced and directed many hits, including *Dil To Pagal Hai* (1997) and *Veer-Zaara* (2004), and he helped launch the career of stars such as Amitabh Bachchan (see pages 104–105).

◀ **John Lasseter** Groundbreaking computer-generated animations from Pixar have changed animation forever, and the man behind many of Pixar's greatest hits is John Lasseter. In addition to overseeing all Pixar productions, he has been a driving force in the development of new technologies and has directed films such as *Toy Story* (1995) and *Cars* (2006).

John Lasseter at the London premiere of *Cars 2* (2011)

▶ **Didier Brunner** If you think only Disney makes great animated features, you have probably never seen a Brunner film. This French producer has collaborated with directors such as Sylvian Chomet and Michel Ocelot to create movies that combine unusual characters with unusual visual styles. *Kirikou and the Sorceress* (1998) and *The Triplets of Bellville* (2003, shown right) are two of his most famous films.

Writing *a movie*

Where does a movie begin? The first stage may be an idea in someone's head that simply won't go away, or a director might read a book and realize that it would be terrific on screen. **To move from thinking to creating, an idea has to be written down as a screenplay.** This is not a finished work like a novel, but a script for filmmakers to develop.

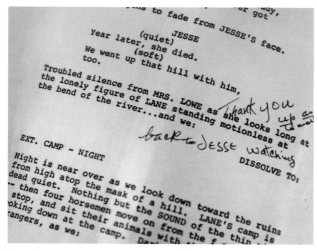

Notes by actor John Wayne on his script from the 1974 movie *McQ*.

Putting ideas in writing

The story to be acted out in a movie is called the screenplay. This document includes the lines to be spoken and briefly describes characters' actions and moods, as well as where each scene will be set. Some screenwriters suggest how scenes can be filmed. The film crew all work from the same screenplay, whether they are actors learning their lines or the director of photography planning the lighting.

The plot hits the spot

It is not just the dialogue that makes a good film. The screenwriter needs to have a plotline that captures the imagination of the filmmakers. Whether the story is a thriller, a comedy, a fantasy, an emotion-filled drama, or all of those at once, the most important thing is that it has the potential to work well on screen.

Life is Beautiful (1997) is a story about a father who protects his son from the horrors of war using comedy.

From book to screen

Turning a book, play, or video game into a film is a big challenge. Some books are full of long descriptions and characters who do more thinking than talking. The novel *Life of Pi*, by Yann Martel, was considered "unfilmable" for those reasons, but the screenplay and spectacular special effects brought the story's magic to life.

Actress Meryl Streep and screenwriter Nora Ephron on the set of *Julie & Julia*

Famous screenwriters

Just as a novelist specializes in writing fiction, some writers make their name with screenplays. Nora Ephron was a journalist, playwright, and director whose screenplays were comedy-dramas bursting with witty one-liners. She wrote 13 movies, including *Julie & Julia* (2009), which was adapted from an unlikely book about cooking.

Snappy dialogue

Everything on the screen is larger than life, and that goes for the lines spoken by the actors, too. For dialogue to come across well in a film, a screenwriter must make conversations between characters sound much sharper and snappier than they would in real life.

There is a lot of slick dialogue in *The Social Network* (2010), a movie based on the founding of Facebook.

The screenplay written by David Magee for *Life of Pi* (2012) was nominated for an Oscar.

Bogart and Bergman in *Casablanca* (1942)

Unscripted

Some famous movie moments are not in the script at all. Nearly everyone quotes "Here's looking at you, kid" as a line from *Casablanca*, but it was originally something that actor Humphrey Bogart said to his costar, Ingrid Bergman, while they were playing cards between takes.

Attention to detail

Getting the look of a movie right takes a lot of hard work. **Costumes, sets, props, and locations** all help set the mood of a film. It is the job of production designers and art directors to take care of every tiny detail, from getting hairstyles right for a historical time period, to keeping track of all the props on set.

On set

Not all movies are shot in the places they appear to be—some are filmed entirely in studios on custom-built sets. Moviemakers go to great lengths to create sets that look convincing. Whole rooms and buildings are constructed, carefully designed to allow for the right lighting and sound recording. They are filled with props that match the feel of the set.

Filming gets underway for *Transformers: Revenge of the Fallen* (2009).

Willy Wonka and the Chocolate Factory (1971) featured a real chocolate river, made from water and chocolate-cream mix. The chocolate cream soured, filling the studio with a horrible smell.

Getting that location

Every movie needs a location manager to find the best places for the story and to get permission to film there. For example, when the crew of *Transformers: Revenge of the Fallen* wanted to film by the pyramids, their location manager had to get special permission from the Egyptian government.

On location

Some places are so spectacular they do not need any help to look good on film. A city or place can be so important to the look of a film that it is almost like another character. Directors like to shoot "on location" when they can, but it comes with challenges. Sound recording is easier on set, and high-profile locations can be hard to gain access to.

La Dolce Vita (1960) was shot in Rome, and featured famous landmarks like the Trevi Fountain.

One place plays another

It is not always possible to shoot a scene as indicated in a script, perhaps because the location is entirely imaginary or a real location is unsafe. New Zealand is a popular location choice for filmmakers, because it has many different dramatic landscapes that can easily stand in for other places.

For the *Lord of the Rings* trilogy, New Zealand's landscape was used to portray the fictional world of Middle Earth.

Cate Blanchett wears an elaborate historical costume in *Elizabeth: The Golden Age* (2007).

Dressing the part

Every costume in a film is carefully planned. A costume reveals a lot about a character—in what period in history they were born, where they live, the kind of job they do, and even what kind of personality they have. Cate Blanchett's costume (above) shows just how important and wealthy her character is.

Edith Head

Possibly the greatest costume designer of all time, Edith Head was nominated for an impressive 35 Oscars, winning eight. Her flattering designs and habit of actually asking actors what they wanted to wear made her a favorite costume designer among the female stars of 1940s and 50s Hollywood. She outfitted many of the most glamorous stars of Hollywood's Golden Age.

Edith Head with some of her Oscars

In the beginning...

The book

After the first Harry Potter book was published (*Harry Potter and the Sorcerer's Stone,* 1997), J. K. Rowling struggled to finish *Harry Potter and the Chamber of Secrets*—because the first book had been so successful, she was afraid the follow-up would not live up to expectations.

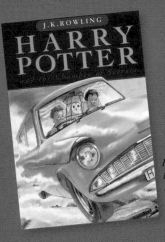

Harry Potter and the Chamber of Secrets, by J. K. Rowling

Young wizards

Many wizards have appeared on screen before Harry Potter. In Disney animation *The Sword in the Stone* (1963), 12-year-old orphan Arthur is taken in and taught magic by Merlin, a kindly wizard, who is a bit like Harry Potter's headmaster Dumbledore.

The cast

J. K. Rowling wanted British children to play the main characters in the Harry Potter movies. Thousands of child actors were auditioned, and the three chosen were Daniel Radcliffe as Harry, Emma Watson as Hermione, and Rupert Grint as Ron. They were all 11 in the first Harry Potter movie.

Author J. K. Rowling (second from left) with Daniel Radcliffe, Emma Watson, and Rupert Grint at the premiere for the last Harry Potter film, *The Deathly Hallows: Part 2 (2011).*

Harry Potter *and the* Chamber of Secrets

The **Harry Potter movies** feature Harry, a young, glasses-wearing, orphaned wizard, who has been accepted to Hogwarts, an imposing boarding school for witches and wizards. Based on J. K. Rowling's best-selling books, Harry's adventures with his best friends, Ron and Hermione, have become hugely successful films. *Harry Potter and the Chamber of Secrets* (2002) is the second in the series.

The story goes... Harry and his friends have just begun the new term at Hogwarts when they find a message warning them that an evil wizard named the Heir of Slytherin has opened the Chamber of Secrets, releasing the beast inside.

All around Hogwarts, people begin to turn to stone. When Hermione falls victim, Ron and Harry are determined to discover the identity of Slytherin's heir.

Suspicion falls on Harry and his rival, Draco Malfoy, but then Hagrid, the gamekeeper at Hogwarts, is charged with the crime and sent to prison. Harry does not believe this of his friend, but if not Hagrid, then who? Only a trip to the Chamber of Secrets will reveal the truth.

Costume

Hogwarts pupils all wear a school uniform. The teachers' outfits may look similar at first, but their differences offer more personal insights. For instance, the all-knowing headmaster, Dumbledore, has touches of red on his robes, a floppy hat, and a long white beard.

Dumbledore is the second from the right.

Flying car

When Harry and Ron miss the Hogwarts Express train to school, they decide to use Ron's dad's car, which has been enchanted to enable it to fly, although it looks like an ordinary car on the outside. Unfortunately, Ron has no idea of how to fly the car!

Harry dangles out of the flying car, right in the path of the oncoming Hogwarts Express.

Quidditch

Harry tries to get away from Malfoy in a Quidditch game.

A rough ball game played on broomsticks, Quidditch is the most popular sport in the wizarding world. Harry plays for his school house, Gryffindor, in the important position of "seeker." The seeker's job is to catch a special winged ball called the Golden Snitch. The game ends when the Snitch is caught.

Harry makes his way through the Chamber of Secrets, ready to battle the monster within.

The Hogwarts look

Inside Hogwarts

Hogwarts School for Witchcraft and Wizardry is a castle, with lots of turrets and secret passages. It has a very grand dining hall, but also cozy, homelike dormitories where the students sleep.

The grand hall at Hogwarts was inspired by this 17th-century dining hall at Christ Church College in Oxford.

Stuart Craig

As production designer on all eight films, Stuart Craig was responsible for the look of *Harry Potter*. His work earned him four Oscar nominations and one BAFTA award. Among the new sets he designed for *Chamber of Secrets* are The Burrow, home of Ron's family, the Weasleys, and the Chamber of Secrets itself, a hidden dungeon lined with giant stone snake heads.

Stuart Craig poses in front of the model that was used to create the outside of Hogwarts.

Make believe

Since early screen stars piled on greasepaint and powder, actors have relied on the skills of makeup artists and hair designers to **transform them for the camera**. An actor might spend several hours getting ready for a shoot, with one makeup artist for the face, another for the body, an optometrist for colored contact lenses, and a hair designer for a wig.

Hair and makeup

Once actors are in costume, it is the job of hair designers and makeup artists to get them ready for the camera. All characters are made up to some extent—whether with period styling to make them look like they've stepped out of history, or modern makeup just to make them as beautiful as possible. Less glamorous characters may need special makeup effects to look dirty, sweaty, or sunburned.

Ve Neill

One of the most famous makeup artists in Hollywood, Ve Neill has worked on an amazing array of characters. These include Johnny Depp as Captain Jack Sparrow and his crew of dirty, barnacle-encrusted pirates in the *Pirates of the Caribbean* series, as well as unusually colorful, futuristic makeup for the *Hunger Games* series. Neill has been nominated for eight Oscars for Best Makeup and Hairstyling and has won three.

Under the gold-tinted Afro wig, Beyoncé Knowles's own hair was braided flat and hidden under a special cap.

The makeup artist used false eyelashes and two types of glitter on Beyoncé's eyes.

A 14-carat gold bead necklace and all-gold wardrobe completed Beyoncé's glam look.

Beyoncé Knowles as Foxxy Cleopatra in *Austin Powers in Goldmember* (2002), styled to look like a 1970s starlet.

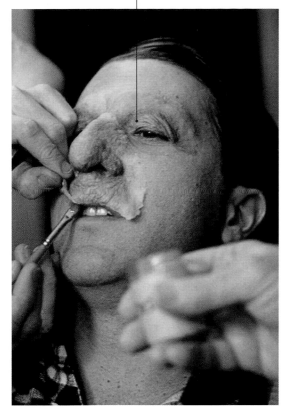

Thin latex layers for the eyelids and mouth are added first, followed by the nose and ears.

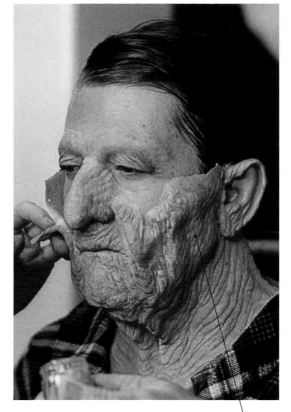

The largest latex pieces are attached to the sides of the face and the neck.

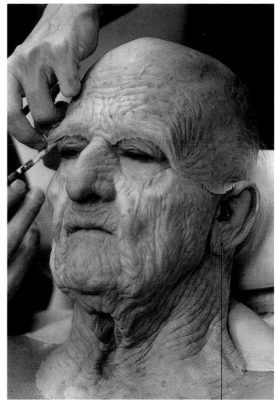

With all mask pieces in place, actor Dustin Hoffman looks decades older.

Special effects

To change the look of an actor completely, a special effects artist first creates a perfect model of the person's face, called a "life mask." Then the artist builds up layers of latex, paint, and hair on this mask to create a full-face "prosthetic." This transforms the actor, who may end up looking like a monster, an alien, or just another person.

Blood and guts

Making an actor appear injured or scarred without hurting them is a careful art. For example, to create the effect of a gunshot to the body, an exploding blood bag, or "squib," is hidden on the actor. When it's pierced, fake blood flies all over the place. Wounds are made with modeling tools, using layers of gel or silicone and different liquid "bloods."

Fake blood comes in many different colors and consistencies.

Johnny Depp as Edward in Edward Scissorhands (1990), with scars made from special gels.

Early effects

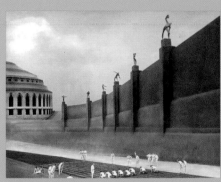

Metropolis (1927)

Schüfftan process This technique relied on the careful positioning of glass and mirrors to make actors look as if they were acting on a huge set. In reality, the set of *Metropolis* was much smaller than it looks here.

The Thief of Bagdad (1940)

Blue screen This technology lets a director add any type of background to a scene. Actors are filmed in front of a blue screen, which is then replaced by the background the director wants. *The Thief of Bagdad* featured early developments in blue screen technology. Today, green screens are more common.

North by Northwest (1959)

Rear projection In this process, actors are filmed in front of a white screen, behind which a projector plays a reversed image of a film. This lets the actor interact with a moving background, like Cary Grant running from the plane in *North by Northwest*.

The world of effects

Filmmakers use a **wide range of special effects** to create the movie magic you see on screen. Techniques vary from simple camera tricks that turn day into night to the use of digital wizardry to create imaginary worlds and impossible creatures. Physical effects are created while filming is in progress, but digital effects are added later. The best special effects often involve a clever blend of both digital and physical techniques.

Matte painting

Spectacular scenery, from futuristic cities to majestic landscapes, is often created by special-effects artists called matte painters. In the past, matte painters worked on sheets of glass, leaving gaps in the painting so the scene could later be combined with filmed action. Today, most matte painters work on computers, often using 3-D graphics so the camera can move through the scene.

This scene is from *The Wizard of Oz* (1939). The background is a matte painting, with a gap in the middle for the characters.

Animatronics

Puppeteer Frank Oz on the set of *The Dark Crystal* (1982).

Monsters and mythical creatures are not always computer-generated. Some are animatronic models— remote-controlled, mechanical puppets that move in a lifelike way. Animatronic models have a motorized skeleton built by engineers and an outer rubber skin finished by makeup artists.

Wind, rain, and fire

Directors can't rely on the weather for their movies and often have to create their own. Rain and wind machines are often used for storm scenes, and fake snow can be made from paper, plastic, foam, or even marble dust, which sparkles like real snow. Fire and explosions are created by licensed explosives experts or faked on a computer.

Fake snow made from marble dust covers a scene in *Doctor Zhivago* (1965).

Films in 3-D

Modern 3-D technology uses the same principles as the first 3-D experiment in 1915. Two cameras record images from different angles: one for the left eye and one for the right. The glasses you wear in the movie theater ensure that syour eyes see these two separate images. Some films are shot in 2-D and converted by computer to 3-D during postproduction, but the effect is not as good as filming in true 3-D.

Hugo (2011) is an adventure film about a boy who lives in a train station in Paris. It was shot entirely in 3-D.

Putting it all together

Many filmmakers blend computer-generated imagery (CGI) with live-action actors or models. It took director James Cameron 500 visual effects and four studios to create the shipwreck in *Titanic* (1997). Large parts of the boat were created in CGI, but a scale model was used for the sinking scene.

Set-builders work on James Cameron's scale model of the *Titanic*

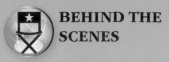
Key creations

1993: Peter Jackson sets up Weta to create horror films.

2001: *The Lord of the Rings: The Fellowship of the Ring.* Weta also worked on the second and third films in the trilogy, which were released in 2002 and 2003.

2004: *I, Robot.* It features thousands of robots in a futuristic Chicago.

2005: *King Kong.* Weapons made for *The Chronicles of Narnia: The Lion, the Witch and the Wardrobe.*

2009: *Avatar.*

2011: *The Adventures of Tintin.*

2012: *The Hobbit: An Unexpected Journey; The Avengers.*

Motion-capture creatures

Creatures that move in an incredibly lifelike way are created by Weta using motion-capture—a process in which an actor's movements are recorded on camera and then transferred to a computer. For example, to create Gollum in the *Lord of the Rings* trilogy, actor Andy Serkis wore a bodysuit covered with reflective dots that produced a map of his body on a computer. Gollum's features were added to this frame to produce a fully animated character.

The character Gollum from *The Lord of the Rings* trilogy appears almost human.

Weta

"I didn't want to make movies, I wanted to make monsters."—Peter Jackson

This **world-famous special effects company** based in New Zealand takes its name from a huge native insect. Weta specializes in creating fantasy worlds on screen and bringing an amazing assortment of creatures to life. The *Lord of the Rings* trilogy and the blockbuster *Avatar* (2009) are among its award-winning productions.

Props and makeup

In the Weta Workshop, which specializes in props and makeup, special-effects artists can create anything from vampires to yetis. Sculptors build scale models of fantasy cities, while engineers and puppeteers bring mythical creatures to life. In *The Water Horse* (2007), a puppet was used to film the scene of the baby Loch Ness Monster splashing in the bathtub. In post-production the puppet was then replaced with a digital version.

In *The Water Horse* (2007), a computer-generated Loch Ness Monster was superimposed on film of a puppet.

Seeing is believing

When a scene with lots of special effects is being shot, what the moviemakers in the studio see in front of the camera bears little resemblance to what we see in the finished film. At the climax of Peter Jackson's 2005 *King Kong*, the heroine, played by Naomi Watts, is held gripped in a giant gorilla's hand high above New York City. The action was filmed against a green screen, with Watts clutched by completely unscary monster green fingers. Later in the production process, a digitally created gorilla hand and city backdrop were merged into the shot.

Digital effects

Weta Digital specializes in CGI (computer-generated imagery) animation, motion-capture, and 3-D filmmaking. Weta used groundbreaking 3-D technology to create humanlike "Na'vi" characters and a beautiful world called Pandora in James Cameron's science-fiction film *Avatar*. This technology was then developed and enhanced to produce *The Hobbit: An Unexpected Journey* (2012) in 3-D.

Avatar features realistic computer-generated characters, such as John Sully, seen here riding a fantasy beast called a great leonopteryx.

Fantasy worlds

When Weta combines its craft and digital skills, there are no limits to the imaginary worlds that can be conjured. Weta can generate lush rain forests inhabited by giant, man-eating insects and dinosaurs, or medieval castles besieged by vast armies created by crowd-generation software. In *King Kong*, motion-capture techniques were used to turn actor Andy Serkis into a 25 ft (8 m) tall computer-generated gorilla.

King Kong protects actress Naomi Watts from the fictional dinosaur *Vastatosaurus rex* in the 2005 version of the movie.

Animation

Since the early days of the movies, audiences have been thrilled by **still pictures or objects coming to life** through animation. To create their magical and imaginative worlds in a short film or feature film, animators today have a wide range of techniques to choose from, including puppets, drawings, actors, music, and computer software.

Silhouettes

Backlighting cardboard cutouts creates characters who are visible only as outlines, or silhouettes. Director Lotte Reiniger pioneered this technique— her 1926 silent film *The Adventures of Prince Achmed* (above) features card cutouts and colored backgrounds. It was based on a collection of folk stories called *Arabian Nights*.

Puppets

The Tale of the Fox (1930) is a story about a crafty fox who tricks a royal lion.

Stop-motion animations are made by moving models slowly and photographing each tiny stage. When the images are shown quickly one after the other, they create the illusion of movement. Animator Wladylsaw Starewicz used puppets for his film *The Tale of the Fox*—he invented mechanisms inside his puppets to give them facial expressions.

With live action

Films do not have to be totally animated or fully live-action—they can be a mix of the two. In *Jason and the Argonauts* (1963, below), Ray Harryhausen used a technique that involved animating models against a background of live-action film. He designed all the interior metal frames and exterior bodies for the models, including sword-fighting skeletons. The model of the bronze statue, Talos, was 12 in (30 cm) high, but on screen he looked 100 ft (30 m) tall!

Cutouts

In cutout animation, flat shapes made from materials such as cardboard and paper are moved around and photographed between each small movement. For *Hedgehog in the Fog* (1975, above), director Yuriy Norshteyn set cutouts of characters on glass shelves under the camera, and moved them around, recording each image between movements to give a three-dimensional look. The blurry effect of the fog was created using tissue paper.

Lucky and Zorba is a cel animation about a seagull who is brought up by a cat.

Cel

In traditional animation, individual parts of a scene were drawn by hand on sheets of paper, or transparent "cel" (short for celluloid). Since 1990, computers have taken over much of this process, but some directors prefer to keep using the "handmade" look. Enzo D'Alò used watercolors to create the backgrounds for his film *Lucky and Zorba* (1998), which won the audience award at the Montreal International Children's Film Festival in 2000.

Markers attached to actors record their every movement. Some are even attached to their faces, to capture their facial expressions.

To create live performance motion-capture, actors wear suits covered in markers, which are then used to generate the animated characters. These before and after shots are of Tom Hanks in *Polar Expresss* (2004).

Computer generated

Since *Toy Story* in 1995, many other feature films have been made entirely using computers. Most computer-generated animations feature totally made-up characters. However, *Polar Express* (2004, right) used a technique called motion-capture to create animation from real people. Actors were filmed by 70 cameras linked to computers. The data from their movements was then used to create smooth, realistic animated characters. Backgrounds and visual effects such as smoke were added in later.

Getting the shot

"Action!" With this famous call, a film director lets everyone on set know that a scene is ready to shoot. Whether a movie is being made in a studio or outdoors on location, **taking just one shot involves a lot of people besides the actors.** Sound, lighting, and camera technicians work as a team to bring the director's ideas to life and keep everything running smoothly.

Cinematographer James Wong Howe

Perfect sound

Muffled words could easily cause moviegoers to lose track of the plot, so every line spoken by the actors must be recorded clearly. This is the job of a technician called the production sound mixer. If anything isn't clear or background noises ruin the shot, then the mixer (or an assistant known as the boom operator) calls for another take.

On location for the mountaineering drama *North Face* (2008), the boom operator uses a long pole to place the microphone as close as possible to the actors.

Capturing the mood

It's not just the action that makes a great movie scene. Clever camera angles and lighting can turn an ordinary shot into one full of atmosphere. Capturing mood on film is one of the skills needed by the director of photography (DoP), sometimes referred to as the cinematographer. Of all the brilliant DoPs who have worked in Hollywood, few are more admired than James Wong Howe, who worked on films from the 1920s to the 1970s, and who used light and shadow to create dramatic effects.

A tracking shot captures an emotional moment on the set of *Exodus* (1960).

Actors on set

Once in costume and makeup, actors place themselves in precise spots on set. They must think about both what they are doing as characters and where the camera is pointing, but the director will guide them through the scene. After the main shoot, actors often do what are called "pickup" shots, when details are filmed separately. They may also have to rerecord some of their lines to improve the dialogue.

Going for a take!

When all is ready, the assistant director (AD) calls "Roll sound!" to start off the sound recordist, and "Roll camera!" to the camera operator. The next order—"Mark it!"—is for the clapperboard operator, who has a hinged board on which the scene and take number are written. Holding the board up to the camera, the operator claps it while calling out the numbers. When the film is edited, matching the "clap" to the camera shot ensures that sound and action recordings can be synchronized.

Jennifer Lawrence waits for the clapperboard on the set of *The Hunger Games* (2012).

Foley sounds

Footsteps, creaky doors, gusts of wind, rockets taking off—when you hear sound effects like these in a movie they have been added in by a sound editor. Some sounds are recordings supplied by a sound library, but editors often arrange for a sound to be specially created in a "Foley studio." Named after Jack Foley, who in the 1920s invented the process of recording sounds in sync with a finished film, Foley artists get the right noise by combining all kinds of surfaces with unlikely props such as shoes, plates, chairs, parts of old cars, and even fruits and vegetables.

A Foley artist at work

Great directors

Behind every great movie is a director with a creative overview of the whole film. With the help of the producer, the director brings all the parts of a film together, decides how to tell the story visually, and directs the actors on set. **Great directors have a distinct style or approach to filmmaking**, which is recognizable whenever you watch one of their movies.

Oliver asks for more food in David Lean's movie *Oliver Twist* (1948).

▶ **Alfred Hitchcock** With his dark sense of humor and instinct for creating tension, Hitchcock was known as the "Master of Suspense." Thrillers like *Vertigo* (1958) and *North By Northwest* (1959) reveal his genius, combining inventive camera shots with intense music and creative editing.

▲ **David Lean** As well as directing two definitive Dickens adaptations—*Great Expectations* (1946) and *Oliver Twist*—Lean made films on a vast scale, such as *Lawrence of Arabia* (1962), an epic packed with blood and battles, panoramic desert scenes, and powerful human emotions.

▲ **Satyajit Ray** Most people think of Bollywood when they imagine Indian movies, but Ray's black-and-white, gently paced films are very different. He worked in many genres, and his coming-of-age films, *The Apu Trilogy*, feature great performances from child actors.

Luc Besson directs aliens in *The Fifth Element* (1997).

▲ **Luc Besson** This French director wanted to be a marine biologist, until he had a diving accident when he was 17. He is well-known for making movies in a style known as "le look," where spectacular visual effects matter more than the storyline. Besson has also directed an animated movie, *Arthur and the Invisibles* (2006), about a small boy and a family of tiny underground people.

Two daughters are locked up by their parents in Samira Makhmalbaf's first film, *The Apple*.

▲ **Samira Makhmalbaf** When she was just 17, Samira, who is also the daughter of a film director, made *The Apple* (1998), one of Iran's most famous movies. A powerful director, her film *At Five in the Afternoon* (2003) was the first to be shot in Afghanistan after a long period of movie censorship.

▼ **Pedro Almodovar** This Spanish director creates colorful films with melodramatic storylines. His work, which tends to feature strong female leads and bizarre goings-on, shows his great ability to direct both tragedy and comedy.

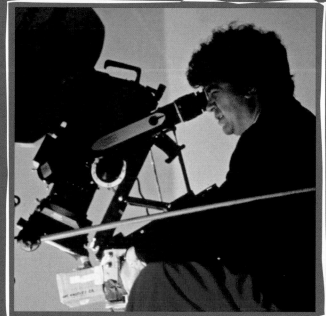

Ousmane Sembène's 2001 film *Faat Kiné*

▲ **Ousmane Sembène** Known as "the father of African film," Sembène gave Africans their own voice in the movies—earlier films were seen through the eyes of Europeans or Americans. His first feature, *The Black Girl* (1966), about a Senegalese girl working as a servant in France, was included in the Cannes Film Festival.

Directors on screen
Some directors cast themselves in movies out of convenience, or because they are also skilled actors. Orson Welles, for example, successfully directed and starred in *Citizen Kane* (1941). Others appear in movies as a joke between the audience and them—you can have fun trying to spot Hitchcock in 39 of his films.

Orson Welles as *Charles Foster Kane*

The Spielberg story

1946: Steven Allan Spielberg is born in Ohio, the eldest of four children. His family later moves to New Jersey, then Arizona.

1958: As a 12-year-old boy scout, he earns his photography merit badge by making a nine-minute Western called *The Last Gunfight*.

1963: At age 16, he makes his first feature-length film, a sci-fi called *Firelight*, which later inspired *Close Encounters* (1977).

1965: Turned down for a place at film school, he begins an internship at Universal Studios.

1968: Directs his first film shown in theaters, the 26-minute *Amblin'*.

1975: Has his first major hit with killer-shark movie *Jaws*.

1994: Founds the studio DreamWorks, which produces hit animations including *Shrek* (2001) and *Kung Fu Panda* (2008).

2011: Earns his seventh Best Director Oscar nomination for *Lincoln*, a biopic of the 19th-century American president.

Boy detective Tintin gets the Spielberg treatment in *The Adventures of Tintin: The Secret of the Unicorn* (2011).

Steven Spielberg

"I like the smell of film. I just like knowing there's film going through the camera."

Creator of some of the greatest—and scariest—science-fiction and adventure movies ever screened, **director Steven Spielberg has won millions of fans**. He is also well-known and much admired for his blockbusters about real people and true historical events. Fact or fantasy, Spielberg knows how to make a story come alive.

Spielberg on set

Getting the best out of both actors and set technicians is what Spielberg is brilliant at. On the shoot for *Indiana Jones and the Last Crusade* (1989), for instance, he expertly handled everything from complicated sequences like a tank chase to touching scenes of a father and son relationship.

Steven Spielberg on set with Harrison Ford in *Indiana Jones and the Last Crusade*

Working with sharks

The movie *Jaws* (1975) is about a killer shark that terrorizes a beach community. Spielberg insisted on shooting scenes in the Atlantic Ocean, instead of in a tank, but, fortunately, did not also insist on real sharks. The one you see in the movie is actually three different life-sized, mechanical models.

A model shark shows some convincing teeth in *Jaws*.

Almost like the real thing—T. rex gets seriously out of control in *Jurassic Park* (1993).

Spielberg as a producer

In addition to directing over 30 movies, Spielberg has been the producer or executive producer on many more. *Men in Black*, a series of movies beginning in 1997, is one of his biggest successes. He persuaded both the lead actors, Tommy Lee Jones and Will Smith, to take part and personally approved the design of the aliens.

Jones and Smith take on aliens in *Men in Black 3* (2012).

Robot dinosaurs

Jurassic Park is about a team of scientists who bring dinosaurs back to life—and, in a way, that's exactly what Spielberg had to do on the film set. A paleontologist (fossil expert) supervised the creation of the animatronic dinosaurs to make sure they looked real. The T. rex's roar was made by combining the sounds of a baby elephant, a tiger, and an alligator.

Bright young
screen stars

To do most jobs, in most parts of the world, you have to be a grown-up, but acting is one of the exceptions to this rule. This is partly because grown-ups dressed as children would look silly in a movie, and partly because many **children are naturals on the screen**. After all, what's acting, if not a giant game of make believe?

Mickey Rooney with Judy Garland in *Babes in Arms* (1939)

▲ **Mickey Rooney** With a career that spans over 10 decades and more than 300 films, Rooney has a special place in Hollywood history. He first appeared in silent movies when he was only a baby, but found real fame opposite Judy Garland, as the title character in 13 *Andy Hardy* movies. He also appeared in a number of musicals, *Babes in Arms* being the best known.

Shirley Temple plays Sara in *The Little Princess* (1939).

▲ **Shirley Temple** Famous for her ringlets, cute smile, and tap-dancing toes, Shirley Temple started acting at the age of three and was a child star by the time she was five. Films like *Bright Eyes* (1934), *Curly Top* (1935), and *The Little Princess* (above) were huge box-office hits but her popularity declined as she grew up.

Romy Schneider as the young
Empress Elisabeth of Austria
in *Sissi* (1955)

▶ **Romy Schneider** Born to a family of actors in Vienna, this German actress first appeared on screen at the age of 15. She shot to stardom at 16 in *Sissi*, a film about the childhood of Elisabeth, or "Sissi," a young princess who becomes the Empress of Austria. Later on, Schneider became a celebrated star of French film.

▲ **Aida Mohammadkhani** Iranian-born Mohammadkhani was seven when she made her debut as a little girl who loses her money on the way to buy a goldfish in *The White Balloon* (1995, above). The film was a hit and she went on to act in other Iranian films, including *Raz-e Mina* (1996).

▲ **Drew Barrymore** Like many child actors, Barrymore comes from a movie business family. With an adorable lisp and blonde curls, she shot to fame as Gertie in the children's science-fiction hit *E.T. The Extra-Terrestrial* (1982, above). She went on to become a big star as an adult.

▲ **Keisha Castle-Hughes** This New Zealand-raised actor is one of the youngest ever to be nominated for a Best Actress Oscar. With no previous acting experience—and only 11 when filming started—she gave a phenomenally moving performance in *Whale Rider* (2002, above), as the Maori girl Paikea "Pai" Apirana, who wants to be a tribal chief.

◀ **Jaden Smith** An actor since he was just six years old, Smith is the son of well-known rapper and actor Will Smith, whose successful career includes both TV sitcoms and major movies. The two Smiths have worked together several times, for example, in *The Pursuit of Happyness* (2006) and *After Earth* (2013). Smith's most interesting role so far is as Dre Parker, a Detroit-born martial arts student in *The Karate Kid* (2010).

Jaden Smith shows off his martial arts skills in *The Karate Kid*.

School on set

You might think that a glamorous career in the movies would mean you could give up classes and exams, but this is not the case. Education for children is compulsory in most countries, which means that child stars can't get out of doing their homework, however famous they become. Movie producers hire an on-set tutor for their young stars, and some child actors attend school in the breaks between their films.

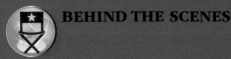

In the beginning…

Albert Lamorisse
Before *The Red Balloon*, Paris-born director Albert Lamorisse was well-known for another short film about a boy with an unusual friend. In *White Mane* (1953) this friend is a wild, white stallion. Lamorisse also directed several documentaries, including Oscar-nominated *The Lovers' Wind* (1978), which was completed by his wife and son after his death in 1970. Lamorisse had another odd claim to fame: he invented the board game Risk.

Short films
The standard length for a feature film is between 70 and 210 minutes. Short films, or "shorts," are movies that are shorter than 70 minutes, and they are often made for children (such as *The Red Balloon*), or as practice for a director who is just starting a film career.

Director's son
The star of this film is the red balloon, but the little boy, Pascal, comes a close second. He is played by Pascal Lamorisse, the nine-year-old son of the director. Pascal did not continue acting after *The Red Balloon*, but later took over his father's film company. His sister, Sabine, also has a role in the film—she plays the girl with the blue balloon.

The **Red Balloon**

This is a magical fantasy story about a little boy named Pascal and his new friend, a red balloon. *The Red Balloon* (1956) is only 34 minutes long, but it has become one of the **best-loved films in children's film**. It won several awards, including an Oscar for Best Original Screenplay, despite the fact that the film has very little actual dialogue in it.

The story goes…
One day, on his way to school, Pascal finds a shiny red balloon. He soon discovers that this is no ordinary balloon. In fact, the balloon is much more like a loyal pet that follows him around wherever he goes. Pascal's stern mother lets the balloon go out of their apartment window, but instead of floating away like an ordinary balloon would, it hovers around outside his bedroom window.

At school Pascal tries to get on with his work, but the balloon follows him into the classroom, causing all the other children to get excited and misbehave. The principal blames Pascal and, as punishment, keeps him locked in his office until school is over.

Later on Pascal and his red balloon bump into a gang of other children who are envious of the balloon. These bullies chase Pascal and finally destroy his balloon. Pascal is sad, but the best surprise is yet to come.

Pascal runs through the cobbled streets of Paris with his red balloon.

Paris on film

The Red Balloon was shot in the Ménilmontant neighborhood of Paris, an area with many narrow alleys, cobbled streets, and steep hills. It seems rather drab compared to the romantic Paris of Hollywood films, and the famous Eiffel Tower is only visible in the distance. This was, however, a deliberate choice by the director Albert Lamorisse. He knew the brilliant red balloon would seem even more magical against this dull background.

Pascal meets a girl with a blue balloon, which seems to have a mind of its own—just like his red balloon.

The flying balloons take Pascal for an enchanting ride over Paris.

The magic of flight

Director Lamorisse turned a plain, faceless balloon into a happy, sad, mischievous friend who follows Pascal everywhere he goes. There were no digital special effects available in 1956, so instead he used very thin thread as well as clever cinematography and editing to make it look as if the balloon had a mind of its own. The balloon itself was specially made for the film and varnished with gloss, to make it look as vibrantly red as possible.

No dialogue, no problem

Silent Movie (1976) makes fun of silent films, with only one word of dialogue in the whole movie.

Silence, please!

The *Red Balloon* is not a silent movie, but it has very little dialogue. Instead, the film uses a lively musical score by Maurice Le Roux, which mirrors the movement of the balloon with odd and enchanting magic. It is not the only dialogue-light film to be made with sound. *Silent Movie* (above) is a comedy that uses visual jokes to make fun of lots of elements of the silent era. *The Artist* (2011) is a more admiring take on silent films, but also uses plenty of music and gestures.

Actor Jean Dujardin (left) won the Oscar for Best Actor for his performance in *The Artist*.

Animal *actors*

Animals have appeared in files since the early days of the movies. Whether as the main star or a friendly sidekick, **animals always make an impression on screen because they are such appealing actors**. Real animals are taken care of by handlers on set, but many movie animals are now animated—so they do not need to be looked after.

▶ *Lassie Come Home*
(1943) Lassie is a loyal, intelligent collie who always comes to the rescue. In *Lassie Come Home* and its six sequels, a male dog named Pal played Lassie. After Pal retired, 10 generations of his descendants starred as Lassie in TV and film spin-offs.

▶ **Storm Boy (1976)**
Mike, nicknamed Storm Boy, prefers exploring Australia's wild coastland to going to school. When a pelican is shot by hunters, he brings up her three chicks and forms a close bond with one he names Mr. Percival. Now Mike must try to protect Mr. Percival from the hunters.

◀ *Black Beauty* **(1994)** A horse who tells his own life story, Black Beauty has some important lessons to teach about kindness to animals. The character was created in a novel by Anna Sewell in 1877 and has been adapted for the movies several times. In this 1994 version, Black Beauty was played by Docs Keepin Time, a former race horse who went on to have a successful career in the movies.

▲ Flipper (1996) Sandy is dreading spending a boring summer with his uncle in Florida, but when he makes friends with a dolphin named Flipper everything gets a lot more fun. Through their friendship, Sandy learns about the environmental threats faced by Flipper and other dolphins.

▲ Babe (1995) Herding sheep is not usually a job for pigs, but Babe is no ordinary pig—he can talk and dreams of becoming a sheep dog. Babe and the other talking animals in this film were created with the help of puppeteers.

▶ Duma (2005)
Xan finds an orphaned cheetah near his home in rural South Africa and decides to raise him. Duma becomes part of the family, but he is soon too big to live with humans. Xan must make an epic journey to take Duma back to the wild.

◀ Hachi: A Dog's Tale (2009) Hachikō was a real dog in Japan in the 1920s, who was famous for being loyal to his master even after his master died. This film relocates the story to the US, but includes all the details, such as Hachikō's nine-year wait for his dead master, and the statue that was built in Hachikō's honor.

Inspiration

Docudrama

The Cave of the Yellow Dog (2005) is a blend of documentary and drama, called docudrama. Director Byambasuren Davaa made the film without a script. This was because she wanted to capture the nomadic lifestyle accurately and encourage the family, all non-actors, to live their way of life as they would normally. It was the introduction of Zochor the dog and Nansal's great friendship with him that gives the film its simple story line and dramatic ending.

Director Byambasuren Davaa (right), during the making of *The Cave of the Yellow Dog*

Nomadic life

Davaa's first film, *The Story of the Weeping Camel* (2003), was also a docudrama. This uplifting movie tells the story of Mongolian shepherds who take care of a camel calf after it has been rejected by its mother. As with *The Cave of the Yellow Dog,* the plot highlights a special bond between humans and animals, and features non-actors displaying the traditions and culture of their rural lives. The movie received an Oscar in the Best Documentary category.

The camel mother with her rare white calf in *The Story of the Weeping Camel*

The Cave of the Yellow Dog

This beautiful tale set in Mongolia is about the special bond between a **young girl, Nansal, and a dog named Zochor**. Their friendship takes place in the spectacular countryside where Nansal's nomadic family lives. The film was made by Mongolian director Byambasuren Davaa and is celebrated for its realistic style and gentle story, which reveals the interaction between rural traditions and the modern world.

The story goes...
Nansal and her family live a nomadic life, moving from place to place with their livestock—sheep, goats, and cattle. One day, Nansal is excited to discover a dog hidden in a cave and names him Zochor, which means "spot." Concerned that the dog will attract wolves, her father tells Nansal that she cannot keep Zochor, but she refuses to listen. When her father goes away to the city to sell sheep wool, the adventurous Nansal gets lost in a storm. She seeks shelter with an elderly woman who entertains her with a magical story about the "Cave of the Yellow Dog," until Nansal's worried mother finds her and takes her home. Soon after, the father returns home with gifts and stories from the city. The family decides that it is time to move to new land. The dog Zochor is tied up and left behind by Nansal's father, much to Nansal's dismay. While making their way to their new home, the family's journey is dramatically halted when they realize Nansal's brother has also been left behind. Surrounded by dangerous vultures, only the dog Zochor is around to help the little boy.

Family photo

The family in the movie are a real-life family—even Zochor the dog is their pet in real life. Large parts of the film show them going about their lives as they do normally.

The family posing for a photo

The sisters riding a motorcycle with their father

A changing life

Nansal and her family live in a countryside that is beginning to interact more and more with the city. Traditionally, the family would have had just enough for their basic needs, but Nansal's father rides to the city on a motorcycle and brings back modern gifts for his family.

Nansal with her best friend, Zochor

Untrained actors

***Kes* (1968)** This movie is about a bullied working-class schoolboy who befriends a wild kestrel (a bird of prey). Despite no previous acting experience, 14-year-old David Bradley was cast in the lead role of Billy, for which he won a BAFTA award.

***L' Argent de Poche* (1976)** This French film (the title means "pocket money") shows children experiencing the challenges of school life and the excitement of first love. Almost the entire cast was made up of nonprofessional actors, including all the children.

***Beasts of the Southern Wild* (2012)** Despite having no previous acting experience, nine-year-old Quvenzhané Wallis became the youngest Best Actress nominee in Oscar history for her role in this film, playing Hushpuppy in a spellbinding drama about a small American community that is threatened by a storm.

Music *on film*

The music that accompanies a film can **really help the story along**—making sad scenes sadder, creepy bits creepier, and battles more thrilling. In the silent era, live music was played along to movies. Today, recorded soundtracks include anything from a newly written orchestral work to a mix of vintage pop songs.

Writing the score

A composer works with a director to write music specific to the actions and emotions of a film, called a film score. Once familiar with the story, he or she can create music that is just right for the action and characters. Composers often bring a unique style to a movie in the same way a director does. For example, John Williams is particularly well-known for his large-scale, swooping orchestral works. He has written some of the most famous film scores of all time, such as the memorable music for *Jaws* (1975) and the *Star Wars* series.

Composer John Williams works with an orchestra to record the soundtrack for *Star Wars: Episode II Attack of the Clones* (2002).

Composer Howard Shore (left) worked closely with director Peter Jackson (right) on the music for *The Lord of the Rings* films.

Special relationship

Directors have strong ideas about how their films should work, so it is important for them to team up with composers who understand what they want. Often, director-and-composer partnerships stay together for several films: for example, director Peter Jackson and Oscar-winning composer Howard Shore collaborated on *The Lord of the Rings* trilogy and *The Hobbit* (2012).

Baz Luhrmann's *Romeo + Juliet* (1996) won a BAFTA award for Best Film Music.

Jukebox soundtracks

Not all soundtracks are newly written orchestral music—they might also be made up of pop and rock tunes that are already familiar. The soundtrack for Baz Luhrmann's *Romeo + Juliet* (above), a modern take on Shakespeare's tragic play, mixes new music with pop songs from the 1990s. Film music sometimes becomes as successful in the charts as the movie is at the box office.

Rock meets film

Since rock 'n' roll legend Elvis Presley's electrifying performance in the 1957 musical *Jailhouse Rock*, audiences have loved seeing famous pop stars in the world of film. Whether playing the role of a singer, like Beyoncé in the musical *Dreamgirls* (2006), or acting in a drama, like Justin Timberlake in *The Social Network* (2010), pop stars use films as platforms to showcase their talents.

Rock icon Elvis Presley performs in *Jailhouse Rock*.

73

Know all about it

Film critics

All you need to be a film critic is to have an opinion about a film. Some people write about films in their free time as a hobby, others turn it into their whole career, writing about movies for newspapers, magazines, or websites. Having seen many films, these critics usually have a vast knowledge of movie history that helps them identify a film's genre and evaluate its plot, style, acting, and direction. Critics can be powerful—positive reviews can boost audience numbers, while negative reviews might cause a movie to flop.

Actor Danny DeVito is interviewed by a young movie enthusiast on the red carpet.

Social media

Websites such as Facebook and Twitter mean that you can upload your thoughts on a movie onto the internet as soon as you leave your theater seat. This makes it easier than ever to get involved in discussions about films. Creating a blog dedicated to the types of movies you want to write about is free and easy to do. There are lots of film blogs dedicated to particular types of films, new releases, or classic films. These blogs make discussing movies from different points of view fun, entertaining, and easy for everyone to take part in.

Spreading the word

How do you find out about a new movie? Is it from your friends, an ad on TV, a poster in a movie theater, a review in a magazine, or a competition on a fan website? **Filmmakers are always on the lookout for audiences,** and they will try anything they can to reach them.

How do movies reach theaters?

Once a feature film is finished, it is a "product" ready to be sold. In many cases, filmmakers work with sales agents who represent them in the global film "market." The agent sells the movie to film distributors in as many countries as possible. Distributors promote the film to movie audiences and DVD buyers, aiming for huge success.

Film posters for *North By Northwest* (1959) in French, Spanish, and Italian

The 2007 Moscow International Film Festival

Film festivals

Held to celebrate moviemaking, film festivals include film screenings and special events such as interviews with directors and award ceremonies. They sometimes focus on a particular genre, or on films from one country. The biggest and bestknown international festivals are the ones held in Cannes, Berlin, and Venice.

Actors dressed as characters from *The Simpsons Movie* at a promotional event for the film

Campaigns

To tempt audiences with a new film and get them into
theaters, film distributors create a marketing campaign.
Usually this includes a poster, a trailer (an ad made up of
clips of the film), and press interviews with the filmmakers.
However, some marketing campaigns go all-out—the big
budget campaign for *The Simpsons Movie* (2007) included
renaming a plane the "Woo-hoo, JetBlue!" in honor of the
character Homer's favorite saying.

Charlie Chaplin with a
model doll of himself

Film merchandise

Merchandise is a product that is made for a film, usually
as part of its marketing campaign. Audiences can buy
toys, clothes, and even food that is connected to the film.
As early as the 1900s, popular characters such as
Charlie Chaplin's "Tramp" have been turned into dolls.
Merchandise builds interest in a film, or keeps it in the
audience's mind long after they have watched the film.

The Red Carpet

At film festivals and ceremonies around the world, performers, directors, and technicians receive awards for being the best of the best. **When film stars arrive at these glitzy events, they walk along "the red carpet," greeting press and fans**. Much the same promotion and glamour surround a film's release.

The Oscars

Since 1929 the Academy Awards have been the most important event in the international film calendar—winning an "Oscar" is a great honor. No one is quite sure where the name "Oscar" came from, but one story has it that the statuette reminded an Academy employee of her Uncle Oscar.

The gold-covered Oscar statuette is 12 in (30 cm) tall.

The Palme d'Or is awarded for Best Film at the Cannes Film Festival.

©A.M.P.A.S.®

And the award does not go to...

The limited number of Oscars on offer means that winning one really is an achievement. Not everyone can win, however, and there are a few surprises on the list of those who have missed out. Despite his long and successful career, Alfred Hitchcock never won an Oscar for Best Director, even though many of his films are still popular today. Actor Peter O'Toole holds the record for receiving the most Oscar acting nominations without ever winning—eight in total, including one for *Lawrence of Arabia* (1962).

Glittering prizes

In addition to the Oscars, there are other awards for filmmakers. The top prize at the Cannes Film Festival in France is the Palme d'Or ("Golden Palm"). It is often considered a key indicator of the year's best film, since it gives equal weighting to non-English-language films. The BAFTAs are Britain's version of the Oscars, and the Golden Bear is awarded to the Best Film at the Berlin Film Festival in Germany. And then there are the Golden Raspberry Awards, or "Razzies." The opposite of the Oscars, they are presented "in recognition of the worst in film."

The Best Film at the Berlin Film Festival wins the Golden Bear.

Celebrities arrive at the Kodak Theatre, California, for the 2009 Oscars.

Award ceremonies

The movie industry eagerly awaits award ceremonies, since simply being nominated for an award can propel any film—or actor—to the top of the box-office charts. They are also an opportunity for stars to show off in glamorous outfits.

Jennifer Lawrence is dressed in style for the 2013 Oscar ceremony.

Quvenzhané Wallis (far right) stars in *Beasts of the Southern Wild* (2012).

Oscar firsts

The Oscars have been running for so long now that their records are hard to beat. It still happens sometimes though—in 2013, Quvenzhané Wallis, age nine, became the youngest person ever to be nominated for Best Actress.

Movies tell **every story imaginable**—from fantastic journeys to action-packed adventures, from romantic tales to real-life documentaries. They can transport you to a time and a place beyond your imagination.

Telling stories

One way of understanding movies is to look at how they tell their stories, based on categories called "genres." Different **film genres include horror, comedy, action, and science fiction.** Each genre usually follows its own rules, which makes it easy to recognize. For example, in certain types of film—say, a road movie—you can expect to see similar characters and much the same sort of settings and action.

How did film genres develop?

Different types of storytelling had long existed in theater and books before filmmakers came along. Some film genres developed thanks to opportunities offered by new technology. For example, the action genre relies on stunts that can only be created with a camera, while road movies must include a car and landscapes—both of which are hard to fit on stage.

Live-action, documentary, and animation

These filmmaking techniques describe different styles. Live-action is when actors are filmed speaking lines. A documentary is a movie of real events, and animation is created with models or drawings. Some movies use computers to combine techniques, such as the live-action and animation mix of the comedy *Alvin and the Chipmunks* (2007).

Alvin and the Chipmunks features singing chipmunks.

Rib-tickling comedy

Comedy is one of the oldest genres—audiences always enjoy a laugh. There are many types of comedy films—for example, slapstick comedies focus on physical jokes such as people falling over and walking into things. "Screwball" comedies focus on fast talking and spoken jokes.

Dr. Dolittle (1998) stars Eddie Murphy as a doctor who can speak to animals.

Fact and fiction

What's real in a movie and what isn't? Digital filmmaking technology and the ingenuity of filmmakers have resulted in new ways of creating illusions and keeping viewers intrigued. Is an actor's face as it appears, or might it have been enhanced with CGI? Is the "real-life footage" in a documentary truly real, or might it have been made up just for the movie?

Spooky horror

Tales of horror, such as the novel *Dracula*, published in 1897, were popular long before the movies existed. Horror films borrow conventions from books—such as dark, stormy nights and supernatural villains. Movies, however, also made new horrors possible, such as gory special effects. The ghost story *The Innocents* (1961) has no gore. Instead, it uses camera angles and shadows to create a spooky atmosphere.

In *The Innocents* the governess is worried by the strange behavior of the children.

In *Howl's Moving Castle* (2004), Grandma Sophie and Howl battle witches and demons.

Genres and countries

If you watch the animation *Howl's Moving Castle* (above), you might guess that it is from Japan. This is because the look of "anime" films, as they are called, is particularly associated with animation made in Japan. Anime characters often have large eyes and colorful or unusual hairstyles. The origins of other genres may be obvious, too. For instance, the Western is firmly located in the Western states of the United States.

Spectacular action

Action movies are all about a hero using physical strength, agility, and mental wit to triumph over difficulties. In the Bollywood film *Dhoom* (2004), for instance, a gang of bikers on a robbing spree try to outwit the law. Despite being popular with fans, action movies rarely win praise from critics, possibly because all the car chases and explosions leave little time for character development.

John Abraham plays the leader of a motorcycle gang in *Dhoom*.

Haywire hybrids

Not every movie fits neatly into one genre, and most films include elements of at least two. Romantic comedy and science-fiction thriller are two common examples of genre hybrids, but there are also more unusual combinations. For example, *Cowboys & Aliens* (2011) tells the story of an outlaw and a wealthy cattleman who team up to save a town from alien abduction. This is an example of the "weird West" hybrid—combining elements of Westerns and science fiction.

Clues to genres

Many elements make up a genre. A science-fiction film will feature advanced technology, spaceships, and ray guns; it will be set far from home, in the future, or on another planet. It will be heavy on special effects to create fantastic new worlds or aliens; the story often features technology versus humans, or good versus evil, and characters will be robots, scientists, or aliens. Science-fiction fans love escapism and drama, so a sci-fi film will have plenty of both.

Animated films

When you watch a modern animated movie, the people, animals, and scenery can look very real, even in a fantasy. The **most convincing movies use computer-generated imagery** (CGI), a technique that is increasingly seen on the screen. Older methods, however, such as hand-drawn images and stop-motion, are still well liked and some animators deliberately return to them.

◄ *The Jungle Book* **(1967)**
Mowgli and his animal friends and foes in *The Jungle Book*—like sly Kaa the snake (left)—are among a long line of characters animated by the Walt Disney Company. The inventor of the feature-length animated musical, Disney loved to explore new ideas. His studio continued to innovate after his death, and was one of the first to include computer animation in live-action films, in the groundbreaking, science-fiction film *TRON* (1982).

► *Toy Story* (1995) Woody the toy cowboy and Buzz Lightyear, a self-important astronaut action figure, shot to stardom when the first CGI feature film, *Toy Story,* was released in 1995. Their creator, John Lasseter, had already made a short CGI film—the Oscar-winning *Tin Toy* (1988)—while working at the computer company Pixar. *Toy Story,* which had Disney's backing, opened up a new world of possibilities for animated films.

◄ *Kirikou and the Sorceress*
(1998) Beautiful designs and a sparky script bring this folk tale to life. The inspiration for the story came from Africa but, like many animated films today, this one was made all around the world. The animation was done in Latvia and Hungary, the backgrounds were painted in Luxembourg, digital coloring was carried out in Belgium, and the soundtrack was recorded in Senegal.

▶ *Wallace and Gromit: Curse of the Were Rabbit* (2005)

Since cheese-loving Wallace and his sidekick Gromit first appeared in *A Grand Day Out* (1989), the original claymation technique used to create them—stop-motion animation of wire-framed clay models—has been enhanced by CGI. In *Curse of the Were Rabbit*, spooky effects like swirling fog were produced digitally.

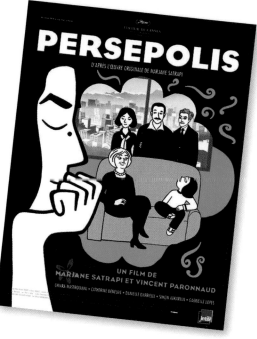

▼ *Shrek* (2001)

In this Oscar-winning animation, the faces of the green ogre, Princess Fiona, and their friend Donkey plainly show their feelings. The production company DreamWorks used new software to create a system of about 500 facial muscle controls, making their CGI characters look astonishingly alive.

▲ *Persepolis* (2007)

There are an incredible 600 characters in *Persepolis*, a film based on Iranian-born French author Marjane Satrapi's autobiographical graphic novel. Satrapi drew all these people in a simple black-and-white style, using such methods as hand-tracing images on paper. She worked with a team of animators and used computer techniques as little as possible.

▲ *Fantastic Mr. Fox* (2009)

The animals in this movie don't move smoothly in the way we now expect of animated characters. This is because when director Wes Anderson made the movie of Roald Dahl's story, he wanted it to have the simple, jerky look of the stop-motion films he loved as a child, and he thought modern audiences would enjoy it, too. Watch out for the movement of the animals' fur, made with artificial and real goat's hair.

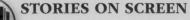

In *My Neighbor Totoro* (1988), two young girls make friends with unusual wood spirits.

Studio Ghibli

This award-winning Japanese animation studio is based in Tokyo. It was established by Hayao Miyazaki, Isao Takahata, and Toshio Suzuki in 1985, and since then has produced around 20 full-length movies. Ghibli productions often feature magical storylines and a cast of fantastical characters, both cute and creepy.

Ponyo (2008) features a goldfish princess who longs to be human.

Spirited *Away*

This magical anime film tells the story of Chihiro, a young girl who finds herself trapped in a **mysterious world full of gods, witches, and monsters**. Getting out of the spirit world is not as easy as getting in, and Chihiro must overcome many obstacles before she can escape.

The story goes... Ten-year-old Chihiro is sulking about moving to a new town with her parents. On the way they take a wrong turn and drive into an abandoned theme park. While her parents eat in an empty restaurant, Chihiro wanders off and meets a boy named Haku. He warns her that she is in danger and must leave before dark, but when she returns to her parents she finds them transformed into pigs. As the spirit world comes to life, Haku takes Chihiro to a bathhouse where she must work—or be turned into an animal by the witch Yubaba. This evil woman changes Chihiro's name to Sen. Haku tells Chihiro that she must remember her real name to keep from becoming a pig like her parents; he then turns into a dragon and flies away. Sen has many adventures in the spirit world. When she captures Yubaba's baby Boh, the witch agrees to release Sen and her parents in return for the little boy. But Sen must pass one last test before she and her parents can be free.

Spirits and monsters

The spirit world is full of strange and unusual creatures. They include frogs who work in the bathhouse, gods who visit to be cleaned, and magic soot balls who work for grumpy Kamajii in the boiler room.

Sen (Chihiro) meets Kamajii, a spiderlike man who runs the boiler room in Yubaba's bathhouse.

Sen (Chihiro) with Haku in dragon form.

In Zeniba's house

Among the characters that Sen (Chihiro) meets in the spirit world is Zeniba, the identical twin sister of the witch Yubaba, who helps Sen to remember her real name. Another spirit is the silent No-face, who wears a spooky mask and can swallow people. No-face learns bad manners from the bathhouse workers, but Zeniba vows to reform him.

Sen (Chihiro) and No-Face, the silent spirit, drink tea with Zeniba.

Awards and acclaim

Spirited Away (2001) is the most successful Japanese animated film of all time. It earned over $274 million at the box office, and has won many awards, including the first Oscar for Best Animated Feature won by an anime film. Other awards include a Golden Bear from the Berlin Film Festival, and Best Film and Best Song at the Japan Academy Awards.

Hayao Miyazaki of Studio Ghibli receives a Golden Lion lifetime achievement award at the Venice Film Festival in 2005.

Tongue twisters

In the English-language version of *Spirited Away* the words were written to match the characters' lip movements. People watching the film in English can't tell that it was originally written in Japanese. This version was created by John Lasseter, the Chief Creative Officer at Pixar and Walt Disney Animation Studios.

The sound of Ghibli

The film score for *Spirited Away* was written by composer Joe Hisaishi and the music was performed by the New Japan Philharmonic Orchestra. The closing song of *Spirited Away,* "Always With Me," with its theme of hopes and dreams, has become much loved both in Japan and elsewhere. The haunting words, originally written for a different movie that was never released, inspired Miyazaki to create the story of Chihiro and her journey from despair to a newfound happiness.

Science fiction

As the name suggests, science-fiction films **mix science and technology with pure fantasy**. Often set in the future or space, they create alternative worlds that capture the viewer's imagination, providing a sense of escape from reality. Alien planets, time travel, robot invasions, and futuristic inventions all feature, making these movies so compelling that sci-fi fans are among the most dedicated movie fans in the world.

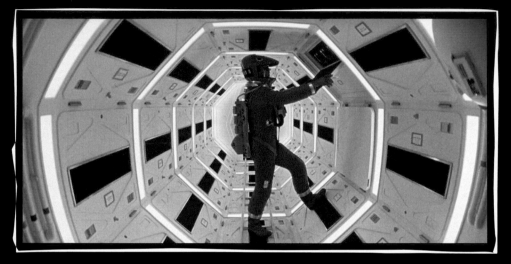

◀ ***2001: A Space Odyssey* (1968)** People have long been fascinated by the idea of outer space. The storyline of *2001: A Space Odyssey* stretches from early man to a future where space travel is common. The movie uses classical music and unusual images to create a sense of wonder. Space travel began in the 1960s and inspired many filmmakers to conjure up futuristic visions of the 21st century.

▶ ***E.T. The Extra-Terrestrial* (1982)** A lonely boy named Elliott finds a wonderful new friend hiding in the woodshed: E.T., an alien who has been stranded on Earth and wants to find a way home. With touching performances from a mostly young cast, Spielberg's blockbuster showed that science fiction does not always have to be action-filled—it can also tell intimate stories of friendship.

◀ ***Back to the Future* (1985)** Teenager Marty McFly is accidentally sent back in time in his professor friend's time-machine car in this first of three films. He can't tinker with events, but he has to make sure his parents fall in love or he will never be born.

◀ ***Metropolis* (1927)** This film is set in a nightmare city of the future where workers are oppressed by machines. Two lovers—Freder and Maria—have their plans ruined by a scary robot. Science fiction often reflects anxiety about new technology. In fact, whenever there is a major scientific breakthrough, a film about its dangers often follows.

▶ The Iron Giant (1999)
Robots can be friendly as well as scary. In this animated film, a nine-year-old boy who has lost his father makes friends with a giant robot that has fallen to Earth from space. The boy tries to hide the robot from the government, which is determined to find and destory it.

▲ The Day After Tomorrow (2004) A popular sci-fi film theme is impending disaster shown on a huge scale. Scientist Jack Hall discovers the climate is cooling. As the planet is plunged into a new ice age, he sets off on a trek across America to find his son. This computer-enhanced film is packed with spectacle and action but has a serious message, since it shows how people must work together to ensure the survival of the human species.

B-movie body snatchers
Movie theaters in the 1950s showed mainstream A-movies with big stars and shorter B-movies that were low on budget but high on creativity. *Invasion of the Body Snatchers* (1956) was a typical sci-fi B-movie about aliens invading a town in California.

◀ Avatar (2009) Director James Cameron's massive international hit *Avatar* uses 3-D technology to immerse the audience in an entirely new world. Humans have come to the lush paradise of Pandora to mine for "unobtainium," without the permission of the blue-skinned Na'vi who live there. Pandora is a utopia, or ideal world, but it is threatened by the behavior of the visiting humans, who put its environment at risk and attack the home of the Na'vi.

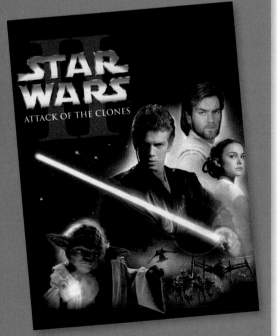

Episode II *Attack of the Clones* sees Anakin Skywalker fall in love.

Star Wars: Episode V
The Empire Strikes Back

A classic battle between good and evil set in a universe teeming with exotic alien civilizations, **the six *Star Wars* films include some of the most stunning science-fiction scenes ever seen**. Episode V *The Empire Strikes Back* (1980) follows on from Episode IV *A New Hope* (1977), in which young Luke Skywalker, with the help of Han Solo, had rescued Princess Leia from the clutches of the evil Darth Vader.

The story goes…
A long time ago in a galaxy far, far away villainous Darth Vader, the leader of the Galactic Empire, is seeking to crush any threat to his power. The resistance against him is led by Luke Skywalker, Princess Leia, and Han Solo. When their base is attacked by Vader's army, the group flees and is separated. Han and Princess Leia are discovered by Vader's men and Han is frozen as punishment.

Meanwhile, Luke crash-lands on a mysterious swampy planet called Dagobah, where he meets an elderly and wise Jedi Master named Yoda. Master Yoda teaches Luke to "feel the Force" and believe that he can defeat the "dark side." Luke's intensive learning of physical and mental powers is interrupted when he discovers that his friends are in trouble, and he rushes to confront Darth Vader. A dramatic lightsaber battle between Luke and Vader climaxes with a surprising discovery for Luke.

Darth Vader

Dressed all in black, with a fearsome helmet and flowing cloak, Darth Vader is one of the most recognizable movie villains of all time. Vader was played by British bodybuilder David Prowse, but his deep intimidating voice was given by American actor James Earl Jones.

Jedi Master Yoda trains Luke Skywalker in the ways of the Force.

Special effects

To achieve his *Star Wars* vision, George Lucas founded a visual effects company called Industrial Light & Magic. It worked on revolutionary and complex techniques that set the standard for big budget movies. For battle scenes on the ice planet Hoth, an artist was hired to paint landscapes and the Imperial Walkers (mechanical vehicles) were shot in front of these landscapes using stop-motion animation. To create Jedi Master Yoda, a puppet was held up by puppeteers, who hid underneath the special sets created for the planet Dagobah in Elstree Studios, England.

Models of four-legged walkers called AT-AT—on screen they looked bigger than buses.

Soundtrack

The music for the *Star Wars* series was written by Oscar-winning composer John Williams. Performed by the London Symphony Orchestra, the powerful and dramatic soundtrack gives the films an epic quality. Some of the "themes" for different characters are now very well-known.

Movie merchandise

In addition to the movies, *Star Wars* has produced a huge number of different products for fans to enjoy and collect. These include action figures, animations, video games, and even themed Lego sets.

Scary *movies*

A scary movie could be a spine-tingling ghost story or a gore-packed zombie thriller—there are as many topics for horror movies as there are human fears. Special effects conjure up all kinds of ghastly goings-on and get more convincing as technology becomes more advanced. Only the best horror movies are still scary years after they were made.

◀ *Werewolf of London* (1935)

Hollywood's Universal Studios established many horror movie conventions and the look of horror monsters such as *Frankenstein* (1931). In *Werewolf of London* (left), Henry Hull plays a scientist who, while on a botanical expedition to Tibet, is attacked by an animal. On returning to London, he begins to transform into a horrifying werewolf.

▼ *The Mummy* (1959)

London-based Hammer Films made science-fiction, thrillers, and comedies, but it is Gothic horror films such as *The Mummy* for which it is most famous. The plots were often borrowed from earlier Universal Studios films, but they shocked censors and thrilled audiences with oodles of Technicolor gore. *The Mummy* is about a murderous ancient Egyptian mummy on the loose in the English countryside.

▶ *Arachnophobia* (1990) Even if

you are not terrified of spiders, the scene where a spider appears in the shower in *Arachnophobia* ("fear of spiders") will make you jump. Natural horror plays on the fear many people have of creepy-crawlies and wild animals. Unlike ghosts and vampires, these scary things actually exist.

▲ *Faust* (1994) "Nightmarish" films are not just

scary—like dreams, they combine the familiar with the unnervingly unexpected. In *Faust*, Czech filmmaker Jan Švankmajer tells the story of Petr Cepek, who stumbles through a nightmare sequence of strange events, beginning with finding a hollow egg inside a loaf of bread.

I scream, you scream

Feeling scared in real life is not fun, so why do we love scary movies? Some scientists think it is because horror films allow us to experience the adrenaline rush (increased heart rate, heightened awareness) of fear, which is similar to excitement. Since we know it is not real and there is no threat to our safety, the relief when we return to our normal lives makes all the unpleasantness worthwhile.

▲ *The Others* **(2001)** It is the things we do not see that are the most chilling. In *The Others*, Grace and her children begin to suspect their remote house may be haunted. The sense of terror is suggested by lighting and music, and suspense.

▼ *Corpse Bride* **(2005)** In horror movies dead things do not often stay buried. Slow-moving and scary zombies are corpses brought back to the real world. Zombie outbreaks are often caused by a virus, but in the animation *Corpse Bride* it is love that sparks Emily's corpse into life.

◀ *Twilight* **(2008)** Edward in *Twilight* is more handsome than the pointy-eared, bald creature in *Nosferatu* (1922), but they are both vampires. Vampires have changed in the last 100 years, but they still suck blood, are cold to touch, and hard to kill. Traditionally they slept in coffins and could not come out in daylight, but the vampires in *Twilight* have overcome these obstacles.

2ND HAND SHOPPE

In the jungle

Tarzan of the Apes

Film studios had been making movies set in the jungle long before *King Kong*. One of the most successful early productions was *Tarzan of the Apes* (1918), the story of an orphan boy who is raised by apes and becomes the human king of the jungle. This first, silent, version of Tarzan inspired many follow-ups.

Tarzan takes a break from swinging through the trees.

The Lost World

Another film that plunged headlong into the jungle was *The Lost World* (1925). This silent movie was adapted from a popular adventure story by Sir Arthur Conan Doyle. The prehistoric creatures were created by special effects man Willis H. O'Brien, who later worked on *King Kong*.

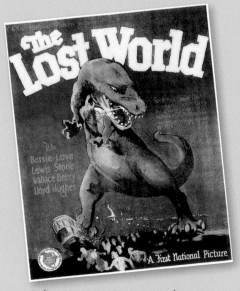

A dinosaur runs riot in an early poster.

King Kong

The giant ape King Kong has roared and rampaged across the screen in several films, but the **original 1933 version** is the one that has had the greatest impact. This movie is remembered not only for the special animation effects that brought Kong to life—an exciting new technique for movie audiences at the time—but also for the touching story. We are terrified by the beast, but we feel sorry for him, too, because he is hopelessly in love.

The story goes… Filmmaker and explorer Carl Denham needs a beautiful leading lady for his latest adventure movie. He finds Ann Darrow in New York and ships her, along with his film crew, to an unmapped island, said to be the home of a mysterious monster. When they arrive, the native islanders kidnap Ann and offer her as a sacrifice to the terrible, godlike Kong, who carries her off to his lair. Denham gives chase, along with ship's mate John Driscoll, who, like Kong, has fallen in love with Ann. After hair-raising exploits in the jungle, they rescue Ann and head back to New York with Kong in shackles as a money-making exhibit. Kong escapes, raging through the streets of Manhattan. He makes a last stand on top of the Empire State Building, Ann in his arms, as military planes close in to shoot him.

Kong's world

Kong's Skull Mountain lair is in the middle of dense jungle on a remote island. This is an alarming world for outsiders, but Kong knows every corner of it. In this scene, he tries to shake his pursuers off a tree bridge over a ravine. As was usual at the time, the filmmakers had little money to build sets, so the jungle scenes were shot on a set shared with another film.

King Kong battles dinosaur Tyrannosaurus rex

Kong versus T. rex

Several of the movie's big action sequences involve King Kong squaring off with prehistoric monsters. When a Tyrannosaurus rex wants to have Ann as a snack, Kong rushes to her rescue. As the giants wrestle, the tree where Kong places Ann for safety is knocked over, but she survives the fall. Eventually Kong kills the dinosaur.

In this clever publicity photograph, King Kong appears to loom over the skyscrapers of New York.

Kong swats a plane out of the sky.

Special effects

Four different-sized Kong models were used in the making of the film. They were created from rubber latex and rabbit fur, with flexible wire to control the great ape's facial expressions as he snarled and bared his teeth. Compared to a real gorilla, Kong's body has a much flatter stomach. That is because the filmmakers thought a Kong with a lifelike protruding pot belly would look ridiculous rather than scary.

More monster movies

Creature from the Black Lagoon

In this classic 1954 horror movie, an expedition group arrives in the Amazon, searching for evidence of prehistoric animals. They assume that a half-man, half-fish "Gill-man" who once lived in the area is now extinct—but is he?

Two different actors played Gill-man, one appearing in the land scenes and the other in the underwater shots.

Godzilla

Japan's answer to *King Kong* was a 1954 movie called *Godzilla*, which features a giant lizard stomping all over Tokyo.

The Day of the Triffids

Based on a novel by John Wyndham, this movie was made in 1962. It is a science-fiction thriller about deadly triffids, giant plants that not only pack a lethal sting but can also walk on their roots to chase after humans.

Actress Janette Scott, playing the wife of a scientist, gets entangled with a triffid.

Martial *arts*

Kung fu and karate are just two of the martial arts—the name given to **traditional fighting skills** using set moves and techniques. These combat arts—thrilling but almost dancelike to watch—are showcased in high-speed, fight-intensive action films, which are usually made in East Asia.

▶ *Drunken Master* (1978)

Mischievous young Wong Fei-Hung (played by Jackie Chan) is always getting into fights, so his father decides to have him trained in a secret martial art called drunken boxing. His tutor is the famous and terrifying Beggar So, otherwise known as Drunken Master. Despite all the fight scenes, this Hong Kong-made movie has plenty of comedy.

▲ *Charlie's Angels* (2000) This film is an adaptation of a 1970s TV show about three tough and beautiful women who use martial arts in their jobs as private investigators. Unlike many martial arts stars, actors Cameron Diaz, Drew Barrymore, and Lucy Liu had no fighting skills, so had to train from scratch, spending months with martial arts expert Cheung-Yan Yuen.

▶ *Shaolin Soccer*

(2001) The monks in the Shaolin Soccer team are not just good at soccer—they are kung fu experts with superhuman skills. Director Stephen Chow enhanced the real skills of his cast with over-the-top special effects, such as a soccer ball kicked into outer space. The cup final of Team Shaolin against Team Evil is a soccer match unlike any other.

Hero features complex choreographed fight scenes.

▲ **Kung Fu Panda** **(2008)** Po the Panda is a kung fu fanatic and idolizes a group of kung fu masters called the Furious Five. Unfortunately, his own martial arts skills are far from masterful. When Po is accidentally named Dragon Warrior, everyone is surprised—it is now up to him to defeat the evil snow leopard. The DreamWorks animators took a six-hour kung fu lesson to help them make the film.

▲ *Hero* **(2002)**
In ancient China a man known only as Nameless (played by Jet Li) arrives at the palace and asks to see the king. He relates the tale of how he has killed the king's three would-be assassins—but is this mysterious man to be trusted? The film is typical of the style known as wuxia, which always includes a gallant, sword-fighting hero.

Stars of martial arts
Many of the most famous martial arts stars are closely associated with a particular style. Bruce Lee was well-known for kung fu films set in modern times, while former ballet dancer Cheng Pei-pei often appears in historical "wuxia" movies, using a dancelike fighting style. Jackie Chan has become an international star in kung fu comedies, which allow him to show his funny side as well as his martial arts skills.

Influences

The wonderful world of wuxia

Wuxia films are martial arts adventure stories set in historical China and often feature fight scenes that defy the laws of physics. Wuxia heroes are highly skilled warriors who live according to a strict moral code. They are the Chinese equivalents of Japanese samurai or English medieval knights. The first ever wuxia movie was a very long Chinese silent film called *The Burning of the Red Lotus Temple* (1928). It lasted an incredible 27 hours in total.

Shaw Brothers

Founded in 1930, the Shaw Brothers Studio released Hong Kong's first film with sound and quickly became Hong Kong's largest movie production company. The studio is best remembered for its martial arts movies and strong female stars, including Cheng Pei-pei, Lily Li, and Tien Niu. Cheng Pei-pei's wuxia film *Come Drink With Me* (1966) was so influential that director Ang Lee decided to cast her as Jade Fox, the main villain in *Crouching Tiger, Hidden Dragon*.

Good and evil

The world of wuxia is often lawless, so in *Crouching Tiger, Hidden Dragon* it falls to warriors such as Mu Bai and Shu Lien to enforce moral order. Wuxia stories also explore the difference between good and evil characters. Often a character is not all bad, but sometimes makes the wrong decisions.

Crouching Tiger, Hidden Dragon

This Oscar-winning martial arts thriller is one of **Chinese cinema's greatest international hits**. It is what is called a "wuxia" film, in which heroic warriors battle on the side of right. *Crouching Tiger, Hidden Dragon* used the money and talents of filmmakers and financiers in Hong Kong, Taiwan, and mainland China. Released in 2000, it paved the way for other wuxia films to become successful worldwide.

The story goes…
In China during the reign of the Qianlong Emperor (1711–99), skilled warriors Li Mu Bai and Shu Lien are in love but won't admit it to one another. Ready to retire from fighting, Mu Bai entrusts his famous sword—the Green Destiny—to Shu Lien and asks her to take it to Peking as a gift for his friend, Sir Te.

When the Green Destiny is stolen from Sir Te's house, suspicion falls on Mu Bai's old enemy Jade Fox and her protégée, Jen. Mu Bai and Shu Lien come together to retrieve the sword, setting in motion a quest that pits friend against friend, student against teacher, and reveals the martial art talents of everyone involved.

Boys versus girls

Tactics and training, not physical strength, are what count in martial arts. The female warriors in *Crouching Tiger, Hidden Dragon* fight alongside the men as their equals. Here, actress Zhang Ziyi shows off her skills.

Re-creating the Qing Dynasty

The costumes and props of *Crouching Tiger, Hidden Dragon* are all based on the Qing Dynasty period of Chinese history, which lasted from 1644 to 1912. The film was shot on location in Beijing and in the expansive Gobi Desert. Careful attention to detail won the movie an Oscar for Best Art Direction.

In this graceful fight scene, Chow Yun-Fat hovers like a bird in the treetops. This was achieved using a technique known as wire-work, where cables suspend the actors in the air.

Ang Lee

Oscar-winning director Ang Lee is not just known for martial arts movies. In fact, it is the variety of his works for which he is most admired. Although his first language is Mandarin, he has directed English-language films in many genres. These include period drama *Sense and Sensibility* (1995), epic adventure *Life of Pi* (2012), and superhero movie *Hulk* (2003).

Sense and Sensibility (1995)

This British period drama is an adaptation of Jane Austen's 1811 novel of the same name, about impulsive Marianne, her sensible sister, Elinor, and the men who want to marry them.

Life of Pi (2012)

Ang Lee shot much of *Life of Pi* in his native Taiwan. Spectacular effects help tell this story about a boy who gets trapped in a boat with a tiger.

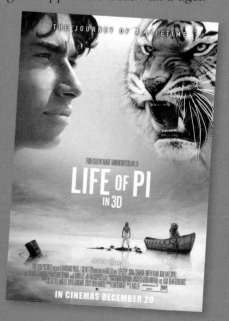

Choreography

Whenever screen characters have to go into action for a dance, a fight, or a crazy chase up and down stairs, their movements are plotted out in exact detail—or choreographed. The actors have to rehearse every part of the sequence again and again to get things right, just as they do with dialogue. The choreographer, who is the person responsible for creating and arranging all the movements, works closely with the movie's director and also with the director of photography.

Busby Berkeley's *Footlight Parade* (1933)

Creating patterns

Some of the early movies contain movement and dance sequences that still raise gasps of admiration. The iconic choreographer of the 1930s was Busby Berkeley, who not only directed huge troupes of dancers, but also filmed them himself. His routines, with dozens of well drilled showgirls creating stunning patterns, have a visual impact equal to anything produced by modern film technology.

A poster for Gene Kelly's music and dance movie *An American in Paris* (1951).

Doing it all

Choreographers must be imaginative, creative, able to turn feelings into movement, and skillful at putting across their ideas to others. Enough talents for anyone—but Gene Kelly, a Hollywood musical movie actor of the 1940s and 50s, had even more. In addition to choreographing his own dances, he was a singer, director, and producer as well.

Dance or stunt?

Dancing in films looks fun, something any of us could do with a little practice. In reality, a big dance number can be nearly as tricky to pull off—and as potentially hazardous—as stunt work, especially when acrobatic jumps and lifts are involved. To avoid chaos, collisions, and leading ladies being dropped on the floor, each sequence has to be carefully choreographed and coordinated, right down to the smallest step.

Choreographed swordplay in *The Mask of Zorro* (1998)

Madhuri Dixit performs a classical Indian dance in *Devdas* (2002).

Fight choreography

Those hand-to-hand fights in action movies may look convincingly spontaneous on screen, but they are choreographed in much the same way as a dance sequence. Whether using swords or lightsabers, fists or feet, actors have to learn their fight moves as precisely as dancers learn their steps. Fight choreographers are usually highly trained in several combat arts.

Bollywood special

Making movies in Bollywood puts a special responsibility on the choreographer. In the West, musicals use songs and dances as interludes in the story, but in Bollywood, dance is essential to the plot. So, whether the style is modern or classical, the choreography must drive the narrative along as well as create spectacular effects.

Nonstop steps

An all-dancing movie makes plenty of work for a choreographer. No one minds a weak plot as long as there is dance, dance, dance all the way through the movie. Whatever the style—and it may be ballet or flamenco, disco or street dancing—every one of the routines has to be prepared in advance.

Street dance routine in *Step Up 2: The Streets* (2008)

Up she goes! This perfectly poised dance lift, seen in the hit movie *Dirty Dancing* (1987), was planned out move by move.

Musicals

When was the last time you saw someone break into a song and dance routine in the middle of the street? It doesn't happen much in real life, but it is an essential part of the action in musicals. Based on the style of musical theater, these feel-good **stories are told through songs, music, and choreography**, and they carry audiences away from their everyday lives.

▲ *The Sound of Music* **(1965)**
To be a star in the golden age of Hollywood musicals, you needed musical talent. In *The Sound of Music*, Julie Andrews shows off her powerful voice playing Maria, the governess who teaches Captain Von Trapp's seven children to sing. The songs from the movie, including "Edelweiss," "My Favorite Things," and the title song "The Sound of Music," remain as popular today as when the movie was first released.

◀ *Singin' in the Rain* **(1952)** Special effects gave Hollywood studios such as MGM the freedom to create spectacular scenes in their musicals. During the title song of *Singin' in the Rain*, Gene Kelly splashes along in torrential rain, created using multiple hoses and sprinklers. MGM had its own, in-house songwriters—if you have a favorite song from a Hollywood musical, it is probably one of theirs.

◀ *Hairspray* **(1988)** In the 1960s-set *Hairspray*, "pleasantly plump" teenager Tracy Turnblad dreams of finding fame in a dance show—until she comes up against racial segregation. It is an example of how musicals started to use original storylines to explore real-life issues, instead of recycling plots and songs from theater.

▲ *Veer-Zaara* **(2004)** Musicals have faded in and out of fashion in Western moviemaking, but in Bollywood they never went away. *Veer-Zaara* tells the story of star-crossed lovers and includes a lot of typical Indian movie music, plus choreography that combines traditional dancing and contemporary Western styles.

◀ *High School Musical* **(2006)** From the 1960s onward, musicals fell out of fashion with the younger generation, but *High School Musical* (shown left) changed all that. In this movie, teenagers Troy and Gabriella discover their love for music at a karaoke contest. This was soon followed by *Mamma Mia!* (2008), which helped make musicals cool again.

▶ *Les Misérables* **(2012)** This movie tells the story of Jean Valjean, a man imprisoned for stealing bread, who is released on parole. He breaks parole and for decades is hunted by Inspector Javert. While avoiding capture, Valjean also agrees to take care of Cosette, the daughter of a factory worker. The story is set in early 19th-century France and is told almost entirely through song, with very little dialogue.

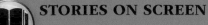

Bollywood
superstars

India is the world's largest producer of films, creating more than 1,200 movies a year in several different languages. Leading the way in popularity and commercial success is Bollywood, the Hindi-language film industry, which is known for its **grand productions filled with colorful song and dance routines**. Many actors try to make it in Bollywood, but only a few achieve superstar status.

◀ **Waheeda Rehman** Classically beautiful and a skilled dancer, Rehman acted in many acclaimed films in the golden age of Indian film between the 1950s and 70s. She first gained recognition with a regional song, which got her noticed by big-time director Guru Dutt. He cast her in several films, including *Sahib Bibi Aur Ghulam* (1962, left).

▲ **Raj Kapoor** One of the greatest entertainers of Bollywood, Kapoor established his studio, R. K. Films, at the age of 24. In 1955 he directed and starred in *Shree 420* (above), playing a character based on Charlie Chaplin's (see pages 16–17) most famous screen persona: the Tramp.

▶ **Aishwarya Rai** This beauty queen was flooded with movie offers after winning Miss World 1994. She has performed in over 40 films, won many Indian film awards, and is often called the world's most beautiful woman.

▲ **Dharmendra** This legendary actor started his career in the 1960s as a romantic hero, but soon made his mark as an action star, earning himself the title of Bollywood's "He-Man." One of his greatest performances was in *Satyakam* (1969), where he plays a young man obsessed with the truth. He enjoyed great on-screen chemistry with many of his leading ladies, including Saira Banu (above in *Aadmi aur Insaan*, 1969).

With the 2002 period film *Devdas* (left), Rai proved that she has acting talent as well as good looks.

▼ **Shahrukh Khan** The "king of romance" began his acting career on television in the 1980s, and made his Bollywood debut in 1992. He was initially noticed for playing "anti-heroes"—leading characters who were far from heroic. Later, he featured in romantic hits such as *Dilwale Dulhania Le Jayenge* (1995). He also starred in a folk-tale movie *Paheli* (2005, below) where he played a ghost who falls in love with a married woman.

▶ **Aamir Khan** This award-winning actor first appeared on screen when he was eight. Over the decades Khan has delivered a string of hits as an actor, producer, and director. These include *Rang De Basanti* (2006, right), which is about a group of students who act in a documentary about the Indian independence movement.

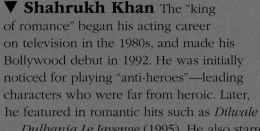

▲ **Ranbir Kapoor** Acting runs in this star's family—his grandfather is the legendary Raj Kapoor, and his parents are both actors. Ranbir Kapoor is known for constantly surprising audiences with his unusual roles. For instance, in *Barfi!* (2012, above), he plays a speech-and-hearing impaired boy who falls in love with an autistic girl.

Beyond Bollywood

Bollywood stars do not just act in Hindi movies. Many feature in lead roles in Hollywood movies. Tabu and Irrfan Khan starred in *The Namesake* (2006), a story of a young Indian in New York City who tries to break away from his family traditions to fit in.

Tabu and Irrfan Khan in *The Namesake*

Amitabh Bachchan

"I don't use any techniques. I'm not trained to be an actor. I just enjoy working in films."

Amitabh Bachchan is India's greatest acting superstar. He has worked constantly since his first film in 1969, acting in more than 180 films and winning many awards. With his baritone voice and tall, brooding good looks, Bachchan has ruled the Bollywood box-office playing action heroes, although he is equally comfortable in romantic comedies and tear-jerkers.

Biography

1942: Born in Uttar Pradesh, India, the son of a famous Hindi poet.

1969: His first movie, *Saat Hindustani,* is released.

1973: Marries actor Jaya Bhaduri. *Zanjeer* is released, launching Bachchan as a superstar.

1975: *Sholay* and *Deewaar* break box-office records and become iconic Indian films.

1976: *Kabhie Kabhie* features Bachchan for the first time as a romantic hero.

1979: Sings on the soundtrack for *Mr. Natwarlal.*

1982: Suffers near-fatal injury while shooting a fight scene for *Coolie*—hordes of fans line up outside the hospital and pray for his recovery.

1990: Wins his first National Award for Best Actor for *Agneepath*.

2000: Debuts on television as the host of the game show *Kaun Banega Crorepati* (*Who Wants to be a Millionaire?*).

2005: *Black* is released to rave reviews, winning him his second National Award.

2009: Wins his third National Award for *Paa*.

Influences

Director Hrishikesh Mukherjee played a crucial role in shaping Bachchan's career, casting him in memorable roles that audiences still enjoy. These include a witty scholar in *Chupke Chupke* (1975) and a complex, introverted man in *Mili* (1975).

Rising star

Bachchan as Vijay, a dockworker who becomes an underworld kingpin, in *Deewaar* (1975)

After a low-key debut in *Saat Hindustani* (1969), Bachchan worked his way through several supporting roles before appearing in *Zanjeer* in 1973. This movie set him up as the "angry young man" of Bollywood, a new type of popular hero who was not afraid to fight authority.

Action rules

Bachchan's popularity skyrocketed with the release of *Sholay* in 1975, a movie that went on to make history as one of the longest-running and most profitable Indian films. It tells the story of two daring young friends who try to help a policeman catch a ruthless bandit.

A poster for *Sholay*, one of Bachchan's first major successes

Beyond movies

In 2000 Amitabh Bachchan began his television career with *Kaun Banega Crorepati*—the Indian adaptation of the UK game show *Who Wants to be a Millionaire?* Bachchan's charismatic and suave style won instant appeal with audiences across the country, making the show a huge success. He won many best TV-anchor awards for the show.

Bachchan hosts *Kaun Banega Crorepati*, a TV game show that gives participants the chance to win huge sums of money.

Amitabh Bachchan plays the aging teacher of a deaf and blind girl in *Black*.

Critical acclaim

Bachchan has brought a wide range of complex characters to life in his long career. He has won three National Awards, including Best Actor for *Black* (2005, shown left). In 2013 Bachchan made his Hollywood debut in *The Great Gatsby*.

Real-life romance

Bachchan has appeared on screen with many women, but his most successful pairing is with Jaya Bhaduri, his wife. They have acted together in many hits, such as *Silsila* (1981), where they play a married couple who are caught in a love triangle. Following in their footsteps, their son Abhishek is also a Bollywood actor.

Amitabh Bachchan acts alongside his wife, Jaya, in *Kabhie Khushi Kabbie Gham…* (2001).

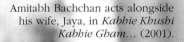

Documentaries

Real life is the starting point for every movie, from musicals to great adventures, but in documentaries it is the star of the show. The first documentary was shown in 1895—a simple film by the Lumière brothers of a train arriving at a station. Since then, documentary-makers have explored **many new and exciting ways of filming and presenting the real world** to bring the stories they want to tell to life.

▲ *Nanook of the North* **(1922)** Years before the word "documentary" was used, this film starred Inuit hunter Nanook at home in Canada's Hudson Bay region. Audiences thrilled at director Robert Flaherty's dramatic scenes of walrus hunting and igloo building, for which he used a combination of real and staged action.

◀ *Night Mail* **(1936)** This poetic film used images, rhythmic verse, and music to tell the story of an overnight mail train carryng letters across the UK from London to Glasgow. John Grierson, one of the filmmakers, was the pioneer who invented the term "documentary."

◀ *Microcosmos* (1996)

Claude Nuridsany and Marie Pérennou, who directed this film, used special cameras to record tiny movements in the grass of a French meadow. Their film is full of mini dramas in the lives of insects: ants are hit by giant raindrops, snails dance, and ladybugs struggle to fly.

◀ *Super Size Me* (2004)

What would happen if you ate only burgers, drank only soda, and avoided exercise for a month? Director Morgan Spurlock did just that to find out if fast food and an inactive lifestyle were making people overweight. He also investigated school meals and doctors' advice, filming his experiment from healthy start to unhealthy finish.

▲ *Être et avoir* (2002) "Fly on the wall"

documentaries observe their subjects from a distance. For this film, called *To Be and To Have* in English, French director Nicolas Philibert filmed a one-room schoolhouse for six months. From 60 hours of film, he created a 100-minute documentary about gaining knowledge and learning how to deal with life, via paint-covered Jojo, his friends, and their families.

Mockumentaries

Comedies presented in documentary style are known as "mockumentaries." With the actors using an unscripted style of acting and the camera sometimes jerky, these films can be brilliant parodies of people taking themselves seriously. For example, *Best in Show* (2000) looks at competitive dog owners.

Jane Lynch and Jennifer Coolidge in *Best in Show*

▲ *Afghan Star* (2009) Reality TV music

competitions are popular all over the world and follow similar formats, though different countries have very different rules. Set in Afghanistan, where music used to be banned, *Afghan Star* follows a singing contest that aims to let Afghan people enjoy music again. The audience, however, is outraged when one of the female contestants chooses to dance while she sings.

Actors in action

You have to be a **certain type of actor to succeed in action movies**. Physical fitness is a must, of course—some stars even do their own stunt work. While there may not be much time for chat, in an action film actors have to be good at delivering short, sharp lines. Many major action stars are associated closely with just one character, who they play in movie after movie.

▲ **Flash Gordon (1936)** A total of 13 *Flash Gordon* films were shown as a serial in US movie theaters, starting in 1936. They starred Olympic swimmer Buster Crabbe as intergalactic warrior Flash Gordon, who battles evil Ming the Merciless to try and save Earth. Crabbe disliked having his hair bleached for the role, so he always covered it with a hat in public.

▲ **Spartacus (1960)** As Spartacus, Kirk Douglas is a man with a more noble mission than many action heroes: he plays an ex-gladiator who leads a slave uprising in ancient Rome. A former wrestler and World War II veteran, Douglas was known for playing military men, cowboys, and other tough guys.

▲ **The Great Escape (1963)** This movie is about a mass breakout of prisoners from a World War II prison camp. Actor Steve McQueen's daring getaway on a motorcycle is one of the most famous chase scenes in movie history. McQueen, an avid car and motorcycle racer in real life, was much admired for his daring and vehicle-handling skills.

▲ **Rocky IV (1985)** Sylvester Stallone didn't just star in the films about boxer Rocky Balboa—he also wrote five and directed four. In *Rocky IV* (1985), the most successful of the series, Rocky comes out of retirement to avenge his friend Apollo Creed, who has been killed in the ring. In the big fight scene, Rocky faces huge Russian boxer Ivan Drago.

▲ **Independence Day (1996)** Earth is threatened by an invasion of hostile aliens, and Will Smith, in the role of US Marine Captain Hiller, volunteers for a dangerous mission. He must gain access to the alien mothership and plant a nuclear missile on board. Audiences warm to the action heroes played by Smith because he brings real-life humor, fear, and bravery to every part.

▶ *Lara Croft: Tomb Raider* **(2001)** Like Indiana Jones, Lara Croft is an archeologist and adventurer whose interest in the ancient world often leads her into danger. Angelina Jolie became famous playing Lara Croft in the movie adaptation of the Tomb Raider video game series. She performed most of her own stunts and went on to appear in many other action films.

▼ *Mission: Impossible—Ghost Protocol* **(2011)** The *Mission Impossible* movies star one of Hollywood's highest paid actors, Tom Cruise. Much respected for his dramatic roles, Cruise is also impressive in these big action films. Playing agent Ethan Hunt, he takes some daring risks on behalf of the fictional espionage organization Impossible Missions Force (IMF).

▲ *The Hunger Games* **(2012)** Jennifer Lawrence went through some tough physical training, including rock climbing and archery, to play feisty heroine Katniss Everdeen in the Hollywood adaptation of *The Hunger Games* novels. The role helped to establish Lawrence as a star.

Stunts on set

Dangling from skyscrapers, leaping on and off speeding trains, stopping a runaway stagecoach: **stunt performers create those "shut-your-eyes" moments** that make action films so spectacular. Clever trickery behind the scenes is often involved, but most movie directors use professional risk-takers, and a few daring actors, to carry out truly dangerous live stunts.

Jackie Chan dangles from a sign high above the ground in *Rush Hour* (1998).

Tom Cruise is suspended from the ceiling in *Mission Impossible* (1996).

How it's done

A finished all-action movie shows only a fraction of the stunt work put into it. Most of the technical side of things is carefully concealed by a special effects team. So that stunt performers can work in safer, controlled environments, stunts are sometimes filmed in a studio against a blank backdrop called a "green screen"; the background scenery for the shot is then added in later. Supporting wires used in flying or falling stunts are airbrushed out of the final film.

Doing it yourself

Not all actors hand their stunts over to specialists—some like to do their stunts themselves. Jackie Chan and Tom Cruise are particularly known for daredevil deeds, whether it is roller-blading under a moving truck or riding a motorcycle through fire. Other actors may be willing to perform, say, a choreographed fight scene, but will use a stunt double when their character gets hurled off a cliff.

Stunt drivers must become very skilled behind the wheels of all kinds of vehicles.

Dangerous driving

Many stunts involve fast-moving vehicles: cars, boats, helicopters, trains, motorcycles. Stunt drivers need super-quick reflexes and extraordinary driving skills to be able to pull off the trick, since even a tiny misjudgement can spell disaster. Stunt cars are specially designed—they have onboard fire extinguishers and roll cages to stop the roof from collapsing when the car flips upside down.

Big bangs

The huge explosions and raging fires we see in movies have to be very carefully controlled so that no real damage is caused. Specialized technical crews release balls of fire and create monster bangs in perfect timing with the action in a scene. If an explosion is judged to be too risky for the actors or stunt performers, it is staged separately and added into the film later. Being set on fire is one of the most dangerous stunts of all—the performer wears many layers of heatproof clothing and there is always a fire safety crew close by.

James Bond skis away from a giant fireball in *The World Is Not Enough* (1999).

Stunt doubles

When a stunt performer stands in for an actor, no one should be able to spot the difference. They look exactly alike and move in just the same way. Some stunt doubles have long careers with their matching actors. Vic Armstrong stood in for actor Harrison Ford on three *Indiana Jones* films. Even people working on set kept getting them confused.

Cameron Diaz (right) with her stunt double, Kimberly Shannon Murphy, during the filming of *Knight and Day* (2009).

Fairy tale *and* fantasy

Across the world, different cultures retell well-known and loved stories in the form of **fairy tales, myths, and legends**. Many of these folk tales have inspired movie adaptations. The characters, dilemmas, and moral lessons of these stories are timeless, and filmmakers can pick and choose which elements to keep and which to update to create new classics.

◀ *The Red Shoes* (1948)
Based on a fairy tale by Hans Christian Andersen about a pair of enchanted shoes, *The Red Shoes* is a story within a story. Moira Shearer plays a ballet dancer who, like the character in the fairy tale, seems possessed by her red dancing shoes.

▲ *The Neverending Story* (1984)
Bastian hides from bullies in the school attic and comforts himself by reading a fairy-tale book, although he soon finds himself inside the story. *The Neverending Story* features dragons, an evil sorceress, and an empress. It surprises the audience with an intriguing twist at the end.

▲ *The Tale of Tsar Saltan* (1966)
This Russian folk tale is about an exiled prince who is helped by an enchanted swan and a singing squirrel. Its director, Alexandr Ptushko, was known for his use of striking and unnatural colors.

Viking Hiccup rides his dragon, Toothless.

Legendary dragons
Fire-breathing dragons are dinosaurlike beasts found in folk stories from different parts of the world, especially medieval England and ancient China. Some movie dragons, like Smaug in *The Hobbit: An Unexpected Journey* (2012), are evil beasts that the hero must slay, but others, like the flying dragon in *How to Train Your Dragon* (2010, left), are more like friendly pets.

▼ *The Hobbit: An Unexpected Journey (2012)* After a visit from the wizard Gandalf (below), young hobbit Bilbo Baggins finds himself swept up into a quest to help a band of dwarves reclaim their lost kingdom of Erebor from a dragon. Their journey takes them over treacherous mountains and through tunnels swarming with goblins, where Bilbo first meets the strange creature Gollum. Fantasy epics such as *The Hobbit* often involve long journeys and make good material for a movie series.

▲ *Azur & Asmar: The Princes' Quest (2006)* This animated film by Michel Ocelot is an "Arabian Nights" inspired adventure tale about two boys who are raised together as brothers. The boys go on a journey to find the Djinn-fairy, but only one of them can be successful in their quest. Ocelet's movies are folklore-influenced stories from around the world, and are so colorful they pop right out of the screen.

▼ *The Princess and the Frog (2009)* Tiana is a hard-working waitress in New Orleans who has been saving up to buy a sugar mill to convert into her very own restaurant. At a ball thrown by her friend Charlotte, Tiana finds herself talking to a frog who is actually a prince under a spell. The movie features voodoo magic, jazz, and a kiss that doesn't quite have the result you might expect—at least not the first time around.

Alice *in* Wonderland

One of the strangest children's stories ever told got a new twist in the extraordinary 2010 movie *Alice in Wonderland*. Director Tim Burton used astonishing computer-generated effects to create a new "Underland" that is both familiar and strange. The original characters are all there, and under the digitally enhanced makeup you will recognize more than a few famous faces.

Tim Burton (left) on the set of *Alice in Wonderland* with Mia Wasikowska

Tim Burton

Director Tim Burton is known and loved for his dark, quirky fantasy films as well as adventurous stop-motion animations for children. The 3-D children's fantasy *Alice in Wonderland* offered him a way to combine these styles. Burton is also known for using the same actors in his movies, for example, Johnny Depp and Helena Bonham-Carter.

The story goes... Thirteen years have passed since Alice first fell down a rabbit hole and began her adventures in Wonderland. Now age 19, she is expected to behave like a young lady and even receives a very unwelcome proposal of marriage at a stuffy garden party. Alice runs off into the woods after a rabbit in a vest and falls down a hole once again. She finds herself back in Underland, the real name for Wonderland, where she is greeted by the White Rabbit, the Dormouse, and twins Tweedledum and Tweedledee. Since it has been foretold that Alice will save Underland from the evil Red Queen's rule, everyone believes she can defeat the Queen's monstrous creature, the Jabberwocky, and restore the good White Queen to the throne. Everyone, that is, except Alice herself.

Being yourself

This older Alice is not happy at joining the grown-up world. In Underland, where everyone behaves strangely, she is free to be herself. There she gains the confidence she needs to stand up for herself.

Alice, played by Mia Wasikowska, looks down the rabbit hole just before falling in it yet again.

The Red Queen

Renowned for her short temper, the character of the Red Queen is based on the Queen of Hearts in Disney's classic musical animated version of *Alice in Wonderland* (1951). Digital effects were used to make actor Helena Bonham Carter's head appear three times its real size.

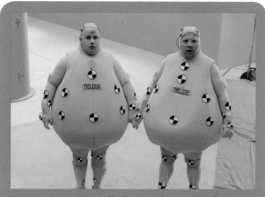

Matt Lucas as Tweedledum and Tweedledee

Green screen

Over 90 percent of the film was shot with a green-screen background, so that the CGI-created Underland could be added in later. This also allowed actor Matt Lucas to play both Tweedledum and Tweedledee, even though they appear on screen at the same time.

Johnny Depp, a regular in Tim Burton's films, plays the wacky Mad Hatter.

Superheroes

Faster than a speeding bullet, the first superhero was "Superman," who shot into a US comic book in 1938. With skills beyond those of any human, these fictional heroes bring us **justice, thrills, some loyal sidekicks, great outfits, and cool gadgets**. Look out for a superhero when all is nearly lost—when the only person who could possibly save humanity would need superhuman skills.

▲ *Superman* **(1978)** In the 1930s, writer Jerry Siegel and artist Joe Shuster created a "superhero" for DC Comics—an alien boy from another planet, Krypton, whose spaceship crashed to Earth. This boy grew up to be Superman, who uses his super powers to battle Lex Luthor and other archenemies for the good of humanity. The first Superman movie was released in 1951, but it was the 1978 version starring Christopher Reeve (above) that catapulted Superman to success and made superhero movies popular.

▲ *Ultraman* **(2004)** Created as a Japanese TV series in the 1960s by Eiji Tsuburaya, Ultraman first appeared on film in 1967. His special powers include the Spacium Ray, which he fires from his right hand to kill enemies. Ultraman is an alien—the timer on his chest flashes to let him know if he is in Earth's atmosphere too long—and he must defeat the *kaiju* (giant monsters) fast.

▲ *Catwoman* **(2004)** DC Comics introduced female burglar "The Cat" in a 1940 Batman comic strip. Dressed in a catsuit and mask, Catwoman has since been both friend and foe to Batman. Halle Berry starred in the only stand-alone Catwoman movie (above); in the film, the heroine uses her feline abilities to seek vengeance.

◀ *The Incredibles* **(2004)** This animated film chronicles the adventures of a family of heroes with super abilities: Helen (Elastigirl), Bob (Mr. Incredible), and their children—shy, teenage daughter Violet (who can turn invisible), son Dash (who is very fast), and baby Jack-Jack, whose powers are yet to be revealed. The family gets forced out of an undercover normal life to fight the powers of evil.

▶ **The Amazing Spider-Man (2012)** In 1962, Stan Lee and Steve Ditko created Peter Parker, a high school student who developed super strength and agility, webshooters on his wrists, and "spider-sense" after being bitten by a radioactive spider. In *The Amazing Spider-Man* he battles "The Lizard," a rogue scientist out to unleash a toxic serum on the world.

Andrew Garfield stars in *The Amazing Spider-Man*.

Christian Bale as Batman riding the batpod, in *The Dark Knight Rises*

◀ **The Dark Knight Rises (2012)** Not all superheroes have super powers. After seeing his parents murdered, millionaire Bruce Wayne declared war on all criminals and became Batman, dedicating his life to fighting enemies of peace. In *The Dark Knight Rises*, the "caped crusader" fights the evil Bane, who is bent on destroying Gotham City.

117

Westerns

Between the 1830s and the early 20th century, thousands of European settlers in the United States headed westward in search of a new life. **Few periods in history have inspired as many movies as those Wild West days.** Since the birth of the movies, moviemakers and audiences alike have loved Westerns. The stories change, but dramatic scenery, gunfights, steely-eyed lawmen, saloon brawls, romance, and lots of horses are almost guaranteed.

▼ *Rio Bravo* **(1959)** This movie is the perfect example of how Hollywood thought the Old West ought to be, with scenes set in the saloons and jailhouse of a dusty frontier town. The characters are types you meet again and again in Westerns: a hardbitten sheriff, played by John Wayne, a lovable drunk (Dean Martin), and a handsome young gunslinger (Ricky Nelson).

▲ *Stagecoach* **(1939)** A group of strangers set off for New Mexico, and the going is tough. They are troubled by outlaws and warring Apaches, and the land is wild and remote. *Stagecoach* was the first of several films director John Ford shot in the vast desert plains of Monument Valley, and it is often mentioned when people talk about great Westerns.

▲ *Once Upon a Time in the West* **(1968)** Westerns are not always all-American. This story of a mysterious stranger and shoot-outs between landowners is a famous "Spaghetti Western." Such movies are so called when the director and many of the crew are Italian. Spaghetti Westerns, often made cheaply and shot on location in Europe, tend to contain lots of action and violence.

▼ *Dances with Wolves* (1990) A soldier wounded in the American Civil War, played by Kevin Costner, finds himself in sole charge of an abandoned frontier fort. He meets and builds up a friendship with the local Native-American Sioux people and is gradually accepted as an honorary member of their tribe. In the old classic Westerns, Native Americans were nearly always portrayed as the enemy, but from the 1960s onward films began to treat them with more respect and understanding.

▲ *Cowboys & Aliens* (2011) In this film, the traditional Western is given a modern science-fiction twist. Set in Arizona in 1873, the story includes typical Western elements such as an outlaw character and a small town terrorized by bandits. Only in this case, the bandits have arrived not on horseback but in a spaceship.

Actor Graham Greene played Sioux medicine man Kicking Bird in *Dances with Wolves*.

John Wayne

Clint Eastwood

This town ain't big enough for the both of us

Actors John Wayne and Clint Eastwood are the most famous cowboys of all. After Wayne's breakthrough performance in *Stagecoach*, his unique style influenced onscreen cowboys, sheriffs, and outlaws—including Eastwood—for the next 30 years. Younger and grittier, Eastwood first appeared in the 1960s TV series *Rawhide*, and he became a star in three Spaghetti Westerns featuring the "Man with No Name."

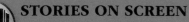

The Real Butch and Sundance

Butch Cassidy

Butch Cassidy was the leader of the most successful American train-robbing gang in history. Born Robert LeRoy Parker in 1866, he was the eldest of 13 children. Cassidy traveled widely around Wyoming, Montana, Colorado, and Texas, robbing banks and ranches before forming his gang, the "Wild Bunch," around 1896. Despite his many recorded crimes, he only served a total of 18 months in prison.

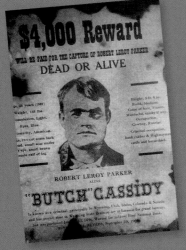

This "Wanted" poster from 1900 was issued after Cassidy robbed the First National Bank in Nevada.

The Sundance Kid

Harry Alonzo Longabaugh, the real Sundance Kid, was born in 1867. At 15, he left home and soon became involved in robberies. He got his name when caught stealing from a ranch in Sundance, Wyoming. After leaving prison, he worked as a cowboy for a while, before joining Cassidy's "Wild Bunch" gang in Wyoming around 1896. Like Cassidy, the circumstances of his death are unknown and his remains were never found.

Sundance was reported to be fast with a gun.

Butch Cassidy *and the* Sundance Kid

Butch Cassidy and the Sundance Kid (1969) has all the cowboys, guns, and lawlessness we expect from a Western movie. However, the story, which is **based on two real outlaws** from the end of the "Wild West" period, is often funnier than it is dramatic, as it mocks the authority figures who chase the charming, daring, and likeable bandit friends played by Paul Newman and Robert Redford.

The story goes… Butch Cassidy and the Sundance Kid are outlaws in late 19th-century Wyoming. When their daring robbery of a Union Pacific train goes wrong, they find themselves on the run from a gang of lawmen. These lawmen have been paid by the train company to capture them—dead or alive, but preferably dead.

With Sundance's schoolteacher girlfriend, Etta Place, in tow, they make a dash for the border, eventually arriving in Bolivia in South America. Butch thinks they have finally found a paradise for outlaws. Sundance, however, is less impressed. With Etta's help, they soon learn enough Spanish to rob banks and become "Los Bandidos Yanquis" (The Yankee Bandits).

Fearing that the Union Pacific lawmen are still on their tail, Butch and Sundance decide to go on the straight and narrow, but after falling victim to a robbery themselves, they return to their old ways. After Etta returns to the US, Butch and Sundance stay in Bolivia for one final robbery, which quickly descends into a gunfight with local lawmen. Will this be the outlaws' last stand? Or will Butch and Sundance live to fight another day?

Iconic song

The song "Raindrops Keep Falling on My Head," which is the soundtrack for the bicycle scene (right), became a big hit.

What happens next?

The severely wounded duo take cover in a building (above) before the final shot of the film—a freeze-frame of the two charging out with guns blazing. The freeze-frame leaves Butch and Sundance's fates uknown—just as the fate of the real outlaws.

The buddy movie

Buddy movies often involve a mismatched pair that put their differences aside to work for a common goal, forming a tight—if dysfunctional—bond in the process. Butch talks a lot but Sundance hardly speaks at all. Butch is full of optimism, but Sundance is more sceptical. They are very different, yet somehow they make the perfect partnership.

Cliffhangers

Many films like to leave us guessing as to what happens next. *Butch Cassidy and the Sundance Kid* is not the only famous movie with an unresolved, or "cliffhanger," ending.

The Italian Job (1969)

The last scene of *The Italian Job* is a literal cliffhanger. The gang is left hanging in a bus off the edge of a cliff, and the audience is left guessing whether the gang will make it out alive. The film ends with lead mobster Charlie trying to save everyone by moving gold bars around in the dangling bus.

Sherlock Holmes (2009)

Keeping the thrills going until the very end, *Sherlock Holmes* finishes with a cliffhanger that suggests Holmes' and Watson's work is not yet done. Discovering that the villain they had been chasing is working with another villain who is still on the run, the movie ends with the detective duo having to reopen the case.

Paul Newman (right) as Butch Cassidy and Robert Redford (left) as The Sundance Kid

Drama

A drama is a **story involving some kind of action or conflict** that must be dealt with. It is not all comedy or all tragedy, but somewhere in between the two. In movies, different kinds of dramas may be based on reality or on a book, or be entirely invented. The characters and settings of a drama might tell us something about the country where the movie was made.

◀ *Ladri di biciclette ("Bicycle Thieves")* **(1948)** Antonio needs a bicycle so that he can work and support his family. When his bike is stolen, he is desperate to get it back. With his young son, Bruno, in tow, Antonio walks the streets of Rome in search of his bicycle—and justice. The director of this Italian film, Vittorio De Sica, hired untrained actors whose lives mirrored his characters' to make his film as close to reality as possible.

◀ *All That Heaven Allows* **(1955)** Wealthy widow Cary falls for her young gardener Ron and is forced to choose between social status and true love when her friends and grown-up children disapprove. The exaggerated plot and over-the-top acting in *All That Heaven Allows* are characteristic of melodrama.

▶ *The Conversation* **(1974)** Loner Harry is a surveillance expert who gets paid to listen to people's conversations. One of his assignments worries Harry enough to make him get involved. This psychological thriller keeps us on the edge of the seat for the whole movie with characters whose true intentions remain mysterious.

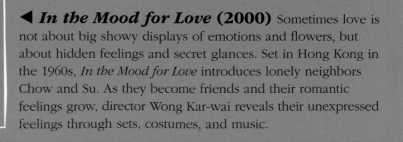

◀ *In the Mood for Love* **(2000)** Sometimes love is not about big showy displays of emotions and flowers, but about hidden feelings and secret glances. Set in Hong Kong in the 1960s, *In the Mood for Love* introduces lonely neighbors Chow and Su. As they become friends and their romantic feelings grow, director Wong Kar-wai reveals their unexpressed feelings through sets, costumes, and music.

▼ *Pride and Prejudice* (2005)

Period dramas use costumes and sets to bring historical eras to life on screen. Adapted from Jane Austen's 1813 novel, *Pride and Prejudice* features Keira Knightley as Elizabeth Bennet, a sensible heroine who is courted by the wealthy Mr. Darcy. Their gradual courtship involves formal balls and dancing, 18th-century dresses, and restrained conversations.

▶ *La Vie en Rose* (2007)

This movie tells the life story of French singer Edith Piaf. It flashes back and forth between her difficult childhood on the streets of Paris and her last days as a prematurely frail 47 year old. Biopics like this follow the history of a real person, often over the course of many years, so they are considered a particular challenge for actors, as well as for special effects, makeup, and costume.

Jodie *Foster*

"Normal is not something to aspire to, it's something to get away from."

Biography

1962: Born Alicia Christian Foster in Los Angeles, California.

1965: Debuts on screen at the age of three in a TV advertisement.

1968: Appears in her first TV show, *Mayberry R.F.D.*

1972: Makes her big screen debut as Samantha in the Disney movie *Napoleon and Samantha*.

1976: Plays a worldly-wise nightclub singer in *Bugsy Malone*, which was directed by Alan Parker.

1977: Nominated for Best Actress Golden Globe for her role in *Freaky Friday*, a movie in which mother and daughter swap bodies for a day.

1985: Graduates from Yale University with a bachelor's degree in literature.

1991: Directs her first film, *Little Man Tate*.

1997: Stars as a free-thinking scientist who discovers an extraterrestrial radio signal in the science-fiction film *Contact*.

2001: Directed herself and Mel Gibson in *The Beaver*, about the manager of a toy company.

2013: Gives a memorable speech on privacy after being honored with the Cecil B. DeMille Award for lifetime achievement at the Golden Globes.

Most Hollywood stars love to be in the spotlight, but Jodie Foster is a talented actress who is respected for **doing things her own way**. She began her career as a child actor, and as an adult she has continued to take leading roles in many award-winning films. Determined to work only on films that she loves, she has also protected her private life from the cameras.

Jodie Foster as Tallulah in *Bugsy Malone*. All the parts in this musical gangster film were played by child actors.

A smart kid

From her first appearance at the age of three in a suntan lotion commercial, Foster has never been off the screen for long. Her most memorable characters are scrappy and determined, such as Annabel, the teenager who swaps lives with her mother in *Freaky Friday* (1976), or wise beyond their years, like Tallulah in *Bugsy Malone* (1976).

A strong woman

Foster has played a wide variety of roles but is best-known for a certain type of character: the strong yet vulnerable heroine. These roles include an English teacher in Siam (Thailand) in *Anna and the King* (1999); a mother imprisoned with her daughter in *Panic Room* (2002); and a scientist in touch with alien life in *Contact* (1997). Audiences feel her fear in every crisis but admire her resourceful approach.

Behind the camera

In addition to acting, Foster has directed three movies. In her first, *Little Man Tate* (1991), she also took the leading role of a mother who is fighting to ensure an adequate education for her child-prodigy son.

Foster behind the camera during the filming of *Little Man Tate*

Foster receives the Cecil B. DeMille Award for lifetime achievement at the 70th Annual Golden Globe Awards (2013).

Lifelong achievement

Throughout her lifetime on film, Foster has accumulated many awards. These include two Oscars for Best Actress, as well as a Golden Globe for her life's work so far. She has acted in over 40 films and continues to take both starring and supporting roles.

Foster plays a strong-willed English schoolteacher in Thailand in *Anna and the King.*

125

Comedy

The things that movie audiences find funny have changed over the years, but **film comedies themselves have never been out of fashion**. They differ a great deal in style, with some relying on crazy stunts, others on clever wordplay. But most comedies end happily, and all have the same goal: to leave you laughing and in a good mood.

▲ *The General* **(1926)** In this silent-era classic, Buster Keaton plays a clumsy but clever train engineer who chases after his stolen locomotive on foot, by bike, and by handcar. This is a comedy that relies on slapstick instead of wordplay. Today, Keaton is recognized as a genius of film comedy.

◀ *Duck Soup* **(1933)**
The introduction of sound in the late 1920s gave movie comedians new opportunities to make people laugh. The Marx Brothers were among the first stars to fully explore the comic potential of dialogue. In *Duck Soup* they played politicians and spies in the bankrupt country of "Freedonia."

▼ *His Girl Friday* **(1940)** When mischievous newspaper editor Walter discovers his star reporter (and ex-wife) Hildy is about to remarry, he decides to sabotage her plans by convincing her to cover one last story. This comedy's pace comes from quick-fire dialogue and the hostile yet flirty relationship between the two romantic leads.

▲ *Ghostbusters* **(1984)** In an action comedy that combines wisecracks with supernatural special effects, three oddball New York scientists team up to form a ghost-exterminator business. The trio stumbles on a gateway to another dimension, unleashing an evil force from which they must save the world.

▲ *10 Things I Hate About You* **(1999)** This movie's plot is adapted from Shakespeare's 16th-century play *The Taming of the Shrew*—which shows how far back romantic comedy goes. The romance is in Cameron's wooing of Bianca, and the comedy is that Bianca's father will allow it only if her grumpy sister, Kat, has a date, too.

▶ ***Mary and Max* (2009)** Mary is a lonely little girl in Australia who decides to write a letter to Max, a random name in the phonebook. Max turns out to be a 44-year-old New Yorker with depression and Asperger's syndrome. It doesn't sound funny, but this clay-animated black comedy can make us laugh at life's darker subjects.

▼ ***Bride & Prejudice* (2004)** This Bollywood version of Jane Austen's classic novel *Pride and Prejudice* (1813) updates the story to modern India. Misunderstandings between Lalita and the rich American, Will, end in true love, with plenty of fun along the way and a big dance routine to finish.

Jacques Tati

"The story is better told with pictures, sound and music."

Filmography

1947: *L'École des Facteurs*—The School for Postmen
1949: *Jour de Fête*—The Big Day
1953: *Les Vacances de Monsieur Hulot*—Monsieur Hulot's Vacation
1958: *Mon Oncle*—My Uncle
1967: *Playtime*
1971: *Trafic*—Traffic
1974: *Parade*

Born Jacques Tatischeff in 1907, **French filmmaker Jacques "Tati" wrote, directed, and starred in many films**. In the 1930s he started to develop the innocent, bumbling character of Monsieur Hulot, for which he would become famous. As a director, he is celebrated for his comedy, precise settings, and use of sound, preferring to make only a few films but get them exactly right.

Behind the camera Tati was in control of every aspect of the movies he directed, from script and performance to production design and camera shots.

Unfinished business

After his death in 1982, a short comedy Tati had filmed in 1978 was finally edited together by his daughter, Sophie. The movie *Forza Bastia* (2002) was about a local soccer team. Later, a semi-autobiographical screenplay he had written in 1956 about a not-very-good magician was turned into *L'Illusioniste* (2010).

L'Illusioniste Set in Scotland in 1959, *The Illusionist* was directed by French director Sylvain Chomet. It is an animated feature film focusing on the friendship between a magician and a girl, Alice, who wants to believe in magic.

Life is funny

To get ideas for his films, Tati liked to observe children playing, innocently and with no inhibitions, which he found very funny. He liked to watch adults, too, especially those who thought they were better than others but actually just looked silly, or who were convinced that modern technology was more important than people.

Monsieur Hulot tries to clear the road in *Trafic* (1971).

Silent comedy

Inspired by his early career as a mime artist, Tati shot his movies silently, then added soundtracks later. There was little dialogue in his films. He was very exact about the setting for his stories, and made sure that it was clear without needing to use words. In *Playtime* (1967), the soft, old-fashioned Hulot contrasts with the vast, modern, impersonal office.

Monsieur Hulot surveys the factorylike office floor in *Playtime*.

A promotional poster for Tati's 1949 film *Jour de Fête*

Tati and technology

Jacques Tati made *Jour de Fête* using new color film—a first for French films—but the process did not work. He had to release the movie in black-and-white, and it was not seen in color until 30 years later. Ironically, *Jour de Fête* is about technology—François the postman is inspired by a news story about how fast modern postal service is in the US. Chaos ensues when he tries to introduce the new system to his sleepy French village.

Who is Monsieur Hulot?

Monsieur Hulot appears in a total of four Jacques Tati films. Played by Tati himself, Hulot is known by the pipe that hangs out of his mouth, his hat, trench coat, too-short pants, and long umbrella. Leaning forward with a funny jerking walk, he is the quiet, unassuming passer-by that other characters hardly notice, until things start to go wrong.

Monsieur Hulot pokes his head out of a window in *Les Vacances de Monsieur Hulot* (1953).

Detectives and spies

In the murky world of murder, theft, and betrayal, **detectives and spies try to stay one step ahead of the pack**. Most spy movies are set in wartime or during tense stand-offs between countries and offer a glamorous spin on real-life intrigues. Detective movies have fast action and smart dialogue and keep you on the edge of your seat with multiple twists and turns in the plot.

▶ *Mata Hari* (1931)

During World War I, Mata Hari was a beautiful Dutch dancer who doubled as a spy, sending secret wartime information about France to her spymasters in Germany. Swedish actor Greta Garbo took the role in a daring movie that was one of Garbo's most successful. It follows the events leading up to Mata Hari's execution for spying.

◀ *The Pink Panther* (1963)

Most movie spies are efficient and slick, so undercover agents who make mistakes can be very funny. In *The Pink Panther*, Inspector Clouseau, famously played by Peter Sellers, is a bumbling detective on the trail of a famous pink diamond. Prone to clumsy mishaps, most of his success in cracking a case comes about by accident.

◄ *Spy Kids 2: Island of Lost Dreams* **(2002)** Sometimes it takes a kid to do a grown-up's job. The heroes of the *Spy Kids* series, Carmen and Juni, are the children of semiretired spies and special agents themselves. In this film, the resourceful siblings work for the child section of the spy agency OSS and get wrapped up in an adventure involving miniature animals and a mysterious "transmooker" device.

▶ *The Bourne Supremacy* **(2004)** The trilogy of Bourne films featuring Matt Damon follow a former CIA assassin, Jason Bourne, who has lost his memory. In the second film, *The Bourne Supremacy,* Bourne is still trying to discover his true identity and is forced to take up his former life as an assassin to stay ahead of his enemies. Bourne is a long way from the smart-talking, sharp-suited spies we often see on screen—he is a gritty, serious hero with a very dark past.

What is film noir?

Film noir means "black film" in French. It is a type of crime movie that is steeped in shadows, from the dark and light you see on screen to the shady motivations of the characters. The kinds of characters that appear in the murky world of film noir are private investigators, policemen investigating dirty dealings, criminals, mysterious women, and hapless citizens who just happen to be in the wrong place at the wrong time. The first film noir movies were made in Hollywood in the 1940s and 50s. They spread worldwide and are still made today.

◄ *Sherlock Holmes* **(2009)** Sir Arthur Conan Doyle introduced the pipe-smoking sleuth Sherlock Holmes in an 1887 novel. He went on to write many novels and short stories about the detective, some of which have been adapted for the screen, including the 2009 film *Sherlock Holmes.* Holmes is the definitive gentleman detective: elegant, confident, and always in control. With his partner Dr. Watson, this master of disguise uses simple powers of observation, logic, and deduction to solve crime.

James Bond

"The name's Bond, James Bond."

Changing Bond

1962: The first Bond movie, *Dr. No*, is released, starring Sean Connery, who made a total of six official Bond films.

1969: George Lazenby makes his only appearance as Bond, in *On Her Majesty's Secret Service*.

1973: Roger Moore plays Bond in *Live and Let Die*, the first of his seven Bond movies, bringing a lighter touch to the role.

1987: Timothy Dalton is a straight-faced Bond in *The Living Daylights*. He made one other Bond movie.

1995: *Goldeneye* is released, starring handsome and hunky Pierce Brosnan. He made three more films.

2006: Ultra-tough Daniel Craig makes the first of three appearances as Bond so far, in *Casino Royale*.

Title sequence

All James Bond movies begin with the same title sequence. Framed by the barrel of a pointed gun, Bond walks on screen, turns, then shoots at the camera, which is slowly covered by dripping blood. The title sequence was originally created by Maurice Binder for the first Bond film, *Dr. No*.

Music

The throb of the Bond theme tune is instantly recognizable. Written by composer Monty Norman, it racks up the tension in many action scenes. The opening credit song to a Bond film usually carries the movie title and is sung by a major star. Madonna sang "Die Another Day" (2002) and Adele wrote and sang "Skyfall" (2012).

Charming, intelligent, ice-cool in the face of danger, James Bond—code name 007—is **the movie's favorite spy**. The British agent for the Secret Intelligence Service (MI6) has a "license to kill" and is sent on special missions to rid the world of evil by his boss, M. The Bond movies sprang from a series of books by Ian Fleming, and they have been thrilling moviegoers for more than 50 years.

Classic Bond

You know where you are with a Bond movie. The pace is going to be fast. There will be someone plotting to destroy a city, a country, or possibly the whole world. There will be explosions and shoot-outs; there may be submarines, helicopters, or nuclear weapons; there will definitely be a thrilling chase. And 007 wins—always.

For each mission, Bond has a fast, stylish, gadget-packed car. The most famous is the Aston Martin DB5, equipped with ejector seats, tire-slicers, and machine guns. It first appeared with Sean Connery in *Goldfinger* (1964).

Actor Donald Pleasence as Bond villain Ernst Stavro Blofeld in *You Only Live Twice* (1967)

The bad guys

At the heart of every Bond mission is a mad scientist or power-driven genius with an evil plan. Famous villains, recognizable by their facial scars, bizarre injuries, and over-the-top badness, include Dr. No, with his metal hands, and evil Ernst Blofield, stroking his white cat as he plots Bond's downfall. Their sidekicks are equally nasty—such as Jaws, a silent giant with metal teeth.

Bond girls

James Bond always meets a beautiful woman, who either wants to help him with his mission or tries to destroy him. "Bond Girls" have exotic names like Honey Ryder and Xenia Onatopp, and they are usually bright, witty, and powerful. Most of them simply can't resist Bond's charm.

Halle Berry as Giacinta "Jinx" Johnson in *Die Another Day* (2002)

Gadgets

No Bond movie is complete without gadgets to help throw the baddies off balance. These can be anything from flame-throwing bagpipes to explosive toothpaste, a bullet-stopping watch, or a briefcase that sprays tear gas if the wrong person opens it. As soon as Bond has his assignment, he visits Q—the quartermaster who issues the spy his gear.

Daniel Craig as a gritty, realistic Bond in *Quantum of Solace* (2008)

Modern Bond

Since Daniel Craig took up the role of Bond in 2006, something different has crept into the films. They are, of course, still full of action, big thrills, and gadgets, but 007 is becoming more believable as a person, showing more real feeling. He is even beginning to wonder whether spying is really a good profession to have.

Playing *with* film

Movies can grab our attention, excite, and surprise us in any number of ways. Since the silent era, filmmakers have played around with film, experimenting to see what new effects they can create and striving to **invent something new and original**. Many of their experimental films don't have large casts. They might be put together very quickly, and they often lack conventional beginnings, middles, or ends.

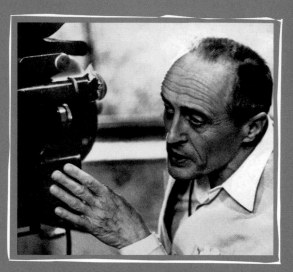

▶ **René Clair** This director enjoyed making movies with dreamlike fantasy elements. His 1924 silent film *Entr'acte* (1924) was based on an experimental ballet and was accompanied by an orchestra. Described by Clair as "visual babblings," the movie featured people running in slow motion, things happening in reverse, an out-of-control coffin, and an egg being shot before transforming into a bird.

◀ ***Rainbow Dance*** **(1936)**
Movies can be used to make information fun. Len Lye made *Rainbow Dance* to promote the British postal service. He filmed a dancer and used the footage to create an outline, which he then overlaid with effects to create "color echoes" dancing to jazz. This combination of elements was like an early version of music videos.

◀ **Norman McLaren** An innovator in animation and abstract filmmaking, McLaren inspired generations of future filmmakers to play around when creating music and images. His experiments included scratching and drawing on the film itself, and energetic, colorful painting on film for *Begone Dull Care* (1960).

▶ ***Meshes of the Afternoon*** **(1943)** This is an experimental movie that is less about what happens on screen and more about how it feels. Created by Maya Deren and Alexander Hammid, the film is dreamlike, with strange, recurring images of a knife and a key, and events are interrupted before they make sense.

▶ ***The 400 Blows*** **(1959)**
The "New Wave" filmmakers of 1950s France made films in a free, expressive, and untraditional style. François Truffaut's *The 400 Blows* sensitively re-creates his own childhood, featuring uncaring parents, nasty teachers, petty crime, but also the value and importance of true friendship.

◄ *The Traveler* (1974) This movie combined documentary and fiction styles to tell the story of Qassem, who funds a 400-mile trip to a soccer game by tricking his classmates into paying for photographs he can't deliver. Its Iranian director, Abbas Kiarostami, later became famous for films like *The White Balloon* (1995).

► *The Wrong Trousers* (1993) Early short films can help filmmakers refine talents that they use in later films. Director Nick Park made this 30-minute clay-animated adventure starring inventor Wallace, his loyal dog Gromit, and evil penguin Feathers McGraw. It showed his skills as a filmmaker and his love of character-led comedy

Short films

Because short films are cheaper and easier to produce than feature-length movies, they often give their creators more creative flexibility. New digital technology has allowed more and more low- or even no-budget films to be made by non-professionals, who are eager to experiment. Some film festivals and websites are dedicated to screening shorts. DVDs often include them as extras to introduce the audience to something new and exciting.

▼ *Thriller* (1983) In the 1980s, music videos became a big deal. For *Thriller*, Michael Jackson worked with a large budget and with John Landis, director of *An American Werewolf in London* (1981). The resulting video is 14 minutes long, looks a lot like a horror movie, and was heavily choreographed. The story features Jackson turning into a zombie, then dancing to his song, along with a whole crowd of other zombies.

So you want to make a movie!

Making your own movie is not impossible. The movies you see at the movie theater may have big action sequences, special effects, and amazing sets, but you should not let that put you off. These days it is easier than ever to get started—all you need are some friends to help you, the right equipment, a bit of free time and, most importantly, a great idea.

Your idea

Think about what type of film you want to make and what story you would like to tell. For inspiration, watch your favorite movies, then brainstorm ideas with your friends. Or you can write about what you already know—think about activities you and your friends enjoy, and make a movie about them.

Planning the action

You have got your team together and have come up with a great idea—the next thing to do is create a storyboard. Split your story into three parts—a beginning, middle, and an end. Then break it down further into scenes. You can plan out each scene using stick figures and diagrams, so that things run smoothly when you start filming.

You don't need fancy props for your movie—simple household objects will work nicely.

Have a look in your closet to see what you can find for costumes.

Props and locations

A "prop"—short for property—is any moveable object used in a film, such as a mug or a pen. Search around your home for anything suitable, and spend a day exploring your area for locations. Think about whether the locations are big enough to use, quiet enough, and safe. Get creative and ask friends if they have anything that could help bring a scene or a character to life.

Costume and makeup

Think about who your characters are, what they would wear, and in what historical period your film is set. You might have a dress-up box at school or some old clothes around the house that you could borrow. You can also experiment with face paint or makeup to change the look of your character—practice in front of a mirror first.

A basic camcorder will work best outdoors.

Using a camera

You don't need big, expensive equipment to make a movie—you can use a phone, a camera, or a camcorder. Just follow these basic rules: keep your hands steady, make sure your actors can be seen clearly before you start recording, and make sure they stay within the frame (the image you see on screen).

Good lighting is important for both live-action and animated scenes. Here models are readied for animation.

Lighting and sound

Good lighting and clear sound will make your movie appear more professional. Natural light is best for filming live action. Make sure your actors are facing the light source, with no shadows falling over the shot. For sound, ensure that the microphone is as close to the actors as possible without being seen, or use microphones that attach to the camera—but be aware that background noise can drown out dialogue.

Action! How to direct

The director has the final say on a film, shouting "action!" to start filming and "cut!" to stop. Be encouraging and positive, and try to be clear when explaining what you want from a scene. Don't be afraid to be creative and try different things.

Prepare for everything

Lights, microphones, and cameras can all create potential hazards. Make sure wires and cables are safely stowed away. If you're filming outside, make a list of everything you think could go wrong while filming so you are prepared for anything.

How to edit

Now that you've shot your footage, it's time to put it together, using your storyboard to remind you what goes where. Software such as iMovie, Windows Movie Maker, and Showbiz DVD can help you edit the film. Try incorporating animation or special effects. Add music and sound effects to take your scenes to the next level.

Showing your movie to your friends is fun.

Getting your film seen

Good job, you've made a movie! Now you need to find an audience. You could even put on a film festival for your friends. Make posters, invite the local press, and sell snacks to raise money. Why not show your film alongside the movies that inspired you?

Glossary

Adaptation A movie developed from the storyline of a play or book.

Animation A technique that brings drawings or models to life by showing a series of slightly different images in quick succession, creating an illusion of movement. Animators may work by hand, use computers, or combine both.

B movie A low-budget feature film, especially of the type made during the Golden Age of the movies to be shown alongside films with major stars.

BAFTA An award given annually by the British Academy of Film and Television Arts for achievements in film.

Biopic A movie that presents a view of a real person's life.

Blockbuster A big-budget film intended to appeal to a wide audience and make a lot of money at the box office. Blockbusters often contain lavish special effects.

Blue screen A special effect where actors are filmed in front of a blue screen and the scene is merged with a different background. Today, using a green screen is more common.

Box office The small booth where tickets were sold in the early days of the movies. Box office also refers to the amount of money that a film makes.

Censorship The removal of scenes from a movie that are considered offensive. Censorship can lead to an entire movie being banned.

CGI (computer-generated imagery) The use of computer graphics to create characters, scenery, and special effects, often in a realistic style.

Cinematographer Also sometimes called the director of photography, this is the lead camera technician in charge of the camera and lighting crews during film production. A cinematographer helps the director create the images and achieve a particular visual style.

Clapperboard A hinged board used to make a clapping sound just before a film shoot starts. This device, also called a slate, helps technicians to synchronize the soundtrack with the images.

Dialogue The words spoken by characters in a film. Dialogue is usually written in the screenplay but may also be made up while a scene is being shot.

Director The person who directs the action on set and is in charge of the overall look and feel of a film.

Distributor The company that markets a movie. The distributor delivers copies of the film to movie theaters and provides stores with DVDs.

Documentary A film that presents a view of real life or actual events.

Editor The person who arranges the film footage in the best order to tell the story.

Feature film A full-length film, usually 80–120 minutes long and always longer than 60 minutes.

Footage The unedited images captured by a camera during filming. The word originates from the traditional measurement of reels of film in units of feet; one foot of film equaled one second of images.

Genre A French word meaning type or category. Many movies can be classified as belonging to a particular genre, such as romance, horror, or science fiction.

Green screen A special effect where actors are filmed in front of a green screen and the scene is merged with a different background.

Live action The use of real actors and settings, rather than animated ones.

New Wave A film movement in France during the 1950s and 1960s. New Wave films rejected Hollywood conventions and featured a distinctive personal approach and visual style.

Oscars The name of the statuettes awarded by the American Academy of Motion Picture Arts and Sciences for achievements in film. The annual ceremony is officially called the Academy Awards but is often referred to as the Oscars.

Postproduction Filmmaking processes that take place mainly after filming is complete, including editing and special effects.

Preproduction Filmmaking processes that take place mainly before filming starts, including casting actors and designing costumes.

Prequel A movie whose story comes before that of an existing movie.

Producer The person responsible for finding the money needed to make a movie and for hiring the main crew, including the director. The producer may also help arrange for distribution of the finished film.

Production The phase of filmmaking in which the actual film is shot. Production involves cast and crew working together on set.

Propaganda Information or ideas spread by movies or other means to support or harm a person, political movement, or nation.

Props Objects used by actors on set or location when acting in a film.

Prosthetics Special effects makeup. False or enhanced body parts are sculpted out of latex and then colored.

Release date The date on which a film can first be seen at the movies or on DVD. A release is often preceded by a lot of promotion.

Screenplay A script written to be made as a film. A screenplay includes dialogue, information about settings, and notes on characters' feelings and camera movements. Traditionally, one page of a screenplay equals one minute of screen time.

Screenwriter The writer of the screenplay, whether original or adapted from a play or book.

Set The scenery and props used as a setting for a film. A set can be interior or exterior, constructed in a studio or on location.

Sequel A movie whose story comes after that of an existing movie.

Series A number of films released one after the other, featuring the same characters.

Shoot "The shoot" is the production stage of a movie. "To shoot" means to film with the camera.

Shot A single view taken by the camera. Different types of shot help tell the story. A close-up, for instance, shows an important detail, while a wide shot can show a whole setting.

Short (film) A short-length movie, usually 5–30 minutes long and always under 60 minutes.

Special effects (SFX) Artificial visual and sound effects created for films, including explosions, green screen, and much CGI work.

Stop motion A traditional animation technique used to film models. The animator reposes the model after each shot, creating a sequence of still images to create the illusion of movement.

Storyboard A series of pictures showing a sequence of camera shots for a scene in a film. Usually based directly on the screenplay, it helps the director and cinematographer plan how best to capture the action and mood of the scene.

Streaming A way of providing films for viewing via the internet or a computer network. Viewers watch the movie while the file is being transmitted, rather than downloading the whole file first.

Studio An organization that makes movies. Also the name for the large buildings and backlots in which film sets are constructed.

Technicolor The brand name for the process used to make the first full-color films in the early 20th century.

Windup cine camera, 1940

Index

Clapperboard

Acknowledgments

Dorling Kindersley would like to thank the following people for their assistance in the preparation of this book: Alice Bowden for proofreading; Helen Peters for the index; Sreshtha Bhattacharya, Vibha Malhotra, Ben Morgan, Esther Ripley, Monica Saigal, and Suparna Sengupta for editorial assistance; Ranjita Bhattacharji, Devan Das, Niyati Gosain, and Tanvi Nathyal for design assistance; Myriam Megharbi for picture research.

FILMCLUB/FILM NATION UK would like to thank the BFI, Eric Fellner, Lord Bichard and First Light.

The publisher would like to thank the following for their kind permission to reproduce their photographs (key: a-above; b-below/bottom; c-center; f-far; l-left; r-right; t-top).

6 The Kobal Collection: MGM (cra); Warner Bros (crb); Dreamworks Animation (br). **8-9 The Kobal Collection:** MGM (c). **10 Dreamstime.com:** Fernando Gregory (tl). **The Kobal Collection:** Georges Méliès (cr); Paramount (crb). **Rex Features:** ITV (bl). **11 The Kobal Collection:** Studio Ghibli / Shinchosha Company (cla); Bonne Pioche / APC / Canal+ / Jerome Maison (cr); Dreamworks (bl). **12 Corbis:** Marco Secchi (cr). **Dorling Kindersley:** The Science Museum, London (cla). **Getty Images:** Science & Society Picture Library (cb). **13 The Kobal Collection:** Georges Méliès (br); Lumière (tr). **14 The Kobal Collection:** Paramount (bl); United Artists (cra). **15 The Kobal Collection:** Hal Roach Studios / Pathe Exchange (cl); Warner Bros (crb). **16 The Kobal Collection:** United Artists / Charles Chaplin (bl); Witzel (tl); First National / Charles Chaplin (cb); United Artists (br). **16-17 The Kobal Collection:** United Artists / Charles Chaplin (c). **17 Alamy Images:** Moviestore collection Ltd (cr). **The Kobal Collection:** United Artists / Charles Chaplin (tc). **18-19 The Kobal Collection:** VUFKU (c). **18 The Kobal Collection:** Pathé (bc); Robert W. Paul (cl). **19 The Kobal Collection:** Goskino (cra, cr, br); Sovkino (tc); Universalia Film (bc). **20-21 Corbis:** Proehl Studios. **21 Getty Images:** Matt Carr (tl); Tim Macpherson (cr). **22 Alamy Images:** Moviestore collection Ltd (bc). **The Kobal Collection:** Universal (cl). **22-23 Mary Evans Picture Library:** Ronald Grant Archive (c). **23 Corbis:** CinemaPhoto (clb). **The Kobal Collection:** MGM (cr); Paramount (ca); DisCina (br). **24 Getty Images:** Redferns / © Disney (tl). **The Kobal Collection:** © Disney (c). **24-25 Alamy Images:** Moviestore collection Ltd / © Disney (b). **25 Alamy Images:** Photos 12 / © 2001 Disney / Pixar (crb). **Dreamstime.com:** Gino Santa Maria / © Disney (c). **The Kobal Collection:** © Disney (tr). **26 Dorling Kindersley:** Museum of the Moving Image, London (bl). **The Kobal Collection:** Universal (c). **27 Begone Dullcare ©1949 National Film Board of Canada. All rights reserved.:** (tr). **The Kobal Collection:** New Line. Ph: Ralph Nelson Jr (crb); 20th Century Fox (tl); Selznick / MGM (cla). **28 The Kobal Collection:** MGM (bl); Chadwick Pictures (cla). **28-29 The Kobal Collection:** MGM (b). **29 Corbis:** Bob King (crb). **The Kobal Collection:** MGM (tl, c); Universal (cr). **30 The Kobal Collection:** Paramount (cra); Warner Bros (cl). **31 Alamy Images:** Moviestore collection Ltd (br). **The Kobal Collection:** Warner Bros. Ph: Jack Woods (crb); Produzione De Sica (tc); Hal Roach / MGM (cra); Daiei (bl). **32 Alamy Images:** AF archive (bl). **The Kobal Collection:** UFA / Karl Ewald (c); Selznick / MGM (tr); United Artists (br). **33 Alamy Images:** Cineclassico (cb); Interfoto (l); AF archive (r). **The Kobal Collection:** Warner Bros (tc). **34 The Kobal Collection:** Duo Films / Arte France Cinema (clb); Filmverlag Der Autoren (tr); Rwa / First Floor Features (crb). **35 The Kobal Collection:** Red Chillies Ent / Eros International / Winford (ca); Warner Bros (cr); Folimage / Digit Anima / France 3 Cinéma (crb); Access Films / MTV Films / Napoleon Pictures. Ph: Aaron Ruell (b). **36-37 The Kobal Collection:** Warner Bros. **38 The Kobal Collection:** Selznick / MGM (bc); United Artists (cb). **39 Corbis:** Splash News (bc). **The Kobal Collection:** Columbia (c, cl); Varahonar Company. Ph: Hashem Attar (tl). **40 Alamy Images:** Photos 12 (bl). **The Kobal Collection:** Sony (cl). **41 Alamy Images:** Adam Eastland Rome (b); Ron Buskirk (ca). **The Kobal Collection:** Oberon / Vela / Wanda (tl). **42 Alamy Images:** Moviestore collection Ltd (cl). **The Kobal Collection:** Amblin / Universal (b). **42-43 The Kobal Collection:** Universal / Working Title (tc). **43 Alamy Images:** AF archive (br). **Corbis:** Splash News (cb). **Getty Images:** (cl). **The Kobal Collection:** Film4 / Pathé / Weinstein-Yuk Films / Goldcrest (cra). **44 Corbis:** Mark Rightmire / ZUMA Press (cl). **The Kobal Collection:** Melampo Cinematografica / Cecchi Gori (clb). **44-45 The Kobal Collection:** Dune Entertainment / Ingenious Media / Haishang Films (c). **45 The Kobal Collection:** Scott Rudin Productions / Columbia (tc); Columbia (cr); Warner Bros. Ph: Jack Woods (crb). **46 The Kobal Collection:** Paramount (cra); Wolper / Warner Bros (b). **47 Getty Images:** (bc). **The Kobal Collection:** New Line / Saul Zaentz / Wing Nut (cr); Riama-Pathé (tl); Universal / Studio Canal / Working Title (clb). **48 Alamy Images:** Ben Molyneux (cl). **Corbis:** Xinhua Press / Zeng Yi (bl). **TopFoto.co.uk:** Warner Bros (bc). **48-49 TopFoto.co.uk:** Warner Bros (bc). **49 Alamy Images:** Ben Nicholson (cra). **Rex Features:** Jonathan Hordle (br). **TopFoto.co.uk:** Warner Bros (cl, tc). **50 Getty Images:** (bl). **The Kobal Collection:** New Line (br). **51 The Kobal Collection:** 20th Century Fox (br); Cinema Center (tl, tc, tr). **52 The Kobal Collection:** MGM (clb, cr); UFA (tl); ITV Global (cl, bc). **53 The Kobal Collection:** MGM. Ph: Ken Danvers (tr); GK Films / Infinitum Nihil (cla); 20th Century Fox / Paramount (b). **54 The Kobal Collection:** New Line / Saul Zaentz / Wing Nut (bl); Universal / Wing Nut Films (cb, bc); Beacon Pictures / Blue Star Pictures (cr). **55 Alamy Images:** Moviestore collection Ltd (b). **The Kobal Collection:** 20th Century Fox (tr). **56 Alamy Images:** AF archive (tr); RIA Novosti (crb). **The Kobal Collection:** Wladyslaw Starewicz Prod. (cl). **Rex Features:** Columbia Pictures / Everett Collection (b). **57 Alamy Images:** Photos 12 (tl). **The Kobal Collection:** Castle Rock / Shangri-La Entertainment (cl, br). **58 The Kobal Collection:** MGM (ca). **58-59 The Kobal Collection:** Dor Film / Lunaris Film (b). **59 Corbis:** Science Faction / Louie Psihoyos (br). **The Kobal Collection:** Lionsgate (cr); United Artists (tl). **60-61 The Kobal Collection:** Paramount (c). **60 The Kobal Collection:** ITV Global (cl); Priya (clb). **61 The Kobal Collection:** El Deseo / Ciby 2000 (cra); Gaumont (tl); Mk2 Prods / Makhmalbaf Prods (c); Filmi Domireew (crb); RKO (bl). **62 Getty Images:** (tl). **The Kobal Collection:** Columbia / Paramount / Wingnut / Amblin (bl); Indiana Jones and the Last Crusade © & ™ 1989-2013 Lucasfilm Ltd. All rights reserved / Paramount / Courtesy of Lucasfilm Ltd. (br). **63 The Kobal Collection:** Columbia. Ph: Melinda Sue Gordon (cr); Universal (tr); Amblin / Universal (cl). **64 The Kobal Collection:** 20th Century Fox (cl); ERMA-FILM (br). **Rex Features:** MGM / Everett Collection (tr). **65 The Kobal Collection:** Columbia (cr); Universal (tl); Ferdos Films (tr). **Rex Features:** Newmarket / Everett Collection (cl). **66 Rex Features:** Films Montsouris / Everett Collection (bl). **66-67 The Kobal Collection:** Films Montsouris (c). **67 Alamy Images:** Photos 12 (tl, cb). **The Kobal Collection:** 20th Century Fox (tr); La Classe Américaine / uFilm / France 3 Cinéma (crb). **68 The Kobal Collection:** MGM (c); Warner Bros (bl). **68-69 Alamy Images:** Photos 12 (c). **69 The Kobal Collection:** Warner Bros. Ph: David Bloomer (cr); Universal (cra, ca); Hachiko Grand Army / Scion Films (bc). **70 The Kobal Collection:** HFF / BR / Mongolkino (bl). **Rex Features:** X Verleih / Everett Collection (cl, br). **71 The Kobal Collection:** Cinereach / Court 13 / Journeyman Pictures (crb); Woodfall / Kestrel (tr); Les Films Du Carrosse (cr). **Rex Features:** X Verleih / Everett Collection (tl, c). **72 Rex Features:** Jonathan Player / Star Wars © & ™ 1977-2013 Lucasfilm Ltd. All rights reserved / Courtesy of Lucasfilm Ltd. (b). **73 Alamy Images:** AF archive (tl). **The Kobal Collection:** MGM (cl); 20th Century Fox. Ph: Merrick Morton (cra). **74 Corbis:** epa / Yuri Kochetkov (bc). **The Kobal Collection:** MGM (cra, fcr, cr). **Photo courtesy of Film Nation UK:** (cl). **75 Alamy Images:** ZUMA Press, Inc (t). **Getty Images:** (br). **76 AFFIF:** (bl). **Berlinale:** Ali Ghandtschi (bc). **Dorling Kindersley:** OSCAR statuette is the registered trademark and copyrighted property of the Academy of Motion Picture Arts and Sciences (fbl). **77 Getty Images:** (bl, t). **Rex Features:** FoxSearchlight / Everett Collection (crb). **78-79 The Kobal Collection:** DREAMWORKS ANIMATION. **80-81 Alamy Images:** Everett Collection Historical. **80 The Kobal Collection:** 20th Century Fox (bc); Bagdasarian / Fox 200 / Regency (cr). **81 The Kobal Collection:** 20th Century Fox (tl); Studio Ghibli / NTV / Tokuma Shoten (tr); Yash Raj Films (c). **82 Alamy Images:** Photos 12 (bl). **The Kobal Collection:** © 1967 Disney (cla); © 1995 Disney / Pixar (c). **82-83 The Kobal Collection:** Dreamworks (bc). **83 The Kobal Collection:** 2.4.7. Films (tr); Dreamworks / Aardman Animations (tc); 20th Century Fox (crb). **84 The Kobal Collection:** Studio Ghibli / Tokuma-Shoten / Nibariki (tl); Studio Ghibli / NTV / Dentsu / Toho (clb); Studio Ghibli / NTV / Dentsu / Tohokushinsha Film (bc). **84-85 The Kobal Collection:** Studio Ghibli / NTV / Dentsu / Tohokushinsha Film (bc). **85 Corbis:** EPA / Claudio Onorati (cra). **The Kobal Collection:** Studio Ghibli / NTV / Dentsu / Tohokushinsha Film (tl). **86 The Kobal Collection:** MGM (cla); Universal (cr); Amblin / Universal (cb); UFA (bl). **87 Alamy Images:** AF archive (tr). **The Kobal Collection:** 20th Century Fox (tl, b). **88 The Kobal Collection:** Star Wars © & ™ 1977-2013 Lucasfilm Ltd. All rights reserved / 20th Century Fox / Courtesy of Lucasfilm Ltd. (clb). **88-89 Alamy Images:** Photos 12 / Star Wars © & ™ 1977-2013 Lucasfilm Ltd. All rights reserved / Courtesy of Lucasfilm Ltd. (bc). **89 Alamy Images:** AF archive / Star Wars © & ™ 1977-2013 Lucasfilm Ltd. All rights reserved / Courtesy of Lucasfilm Ltd. (cla). **The Kobal Collection:** Star Wars © & ™ 1977-2013 Lucasfilm Ltd. All rights reserved / 20th Century Fox / Courtesy of Lucasfilm Ltd. (cr). **90 The Kobal Collection:** Hammer (bl); Universal (ca); Hollywood Pictures / Amblin (cr); Heart Of Europe / Lumen / Athenor (cb). **91 The Kobal Collection:** Miramax / Canal+ / Teresa Isasi (tl); Summit Entertainment (ca); Warner Bros. (b). **92 The Kobal Collection:** First National (bl); NFCA (cla); RKO (cb). **92-93 The Kobal Collection:** RKO (bc). **93 Alamy Images:** AF archive (br). **The Kobal Collection:** RKO (tl, tc); Universal (cra). **94 The Kobal Collection:** Columbia. Ph: Darren Michaels (clb); Seasonal Film Corporation (c); Miramax / Dimension Films (br). **94-95 The Kobal Collection:** Beijing New Picture / Elite Group (c). **95 Alamy Images:** Photos 12 (cr). **96-97 The Kobal Collection:** Columbia / Sony (b). **97 The Kobal Collection:** Columbia / Sony. Ph: Chan Kam Chuen (tl); Columbia / Sony (ca); Columbia (cr); Dune Entertainment / Ingenious Media / Haishang Films (br). **98 Getty Images:** Hulton Archive / Stringer (tr). **The Kobal Collection:** MGM (cl). **98-99 The Kobal Collection:** Vestron (bc). **99 Alamy Images:** AF archive (tl). **The Kobal Collection:** Mega Bollywood (tr); Offspring Entertainment (crb). **100 The Kobal Collection:** 20th Century Fox (cr). **Mary Evans Picture Library:** Ronald Grant Archive (l). **101 © Disney Channel:** (c). **The Kobal Collection:** New Line (tl); Yash Raj Films (tr); Universal / Working Title Films / Cameron Makintosh (br). **102 Alamy Images:** Dinodia Photos (tr); Photos 12 (cl). **The Kobal Collection:** B.R. Films (crb); Mega Bollywood (bc). **102-103 The Kobal Collection:** Red Chillies Ent. (c). **103 The Kobal Collection:** Fox Searchlight / Cine Mosaic / Mirabai Films (bc); ROMP / UTV (tr); UTV Motion Pictures (cr). **104 Alamy Images:** Dinodia Photos (c). **The Kobal Collection:** Sippy Films / United Producers (br). **Rex Features:** Jonathan Hordle (tl). **105 Alamy Images:** Dinodia Photos (cla); Photos 12 (tc). **The Kobal Collection:** Dharma Productions (b). **106 Corbis:** John Springer Collection (tr). **The Kobal Collection:** Gpo Film Unit (b). **107 Alamy Images:** AF archive (tr). **The Kobal Collection:** Aria Productions / Redstart Media (crb); Galatée Films / France 2 (tl); Kathbur Pictures / The Con / Studio on Hudson (cl); Castle Rock / Warner Bros.Ph: Doane Gregory (bl). **108 The Kobal Collection:** Bryna / Universal (cl); Universal (cra); Mirisch / United Artists (clb); MGM / UA (crb). **109 The Kobal Collection:** 20th Century Fox. Ph: Claudette Barius (tl); Lawrence Gordon / Mutual Film / Paramount. Ph: Alex Bailey (tr); Lionsgate (cr); Paramount (b). **110 The Kobal Collection:** New Line / Roger Birnbaum. Ph: Bob Marshak (tr); Paramount (cl); TF1 Films Production (br). **111 Getty Images:** Twentieth Century Fox Film Corporation / Regency Enterprises (bl). **The Kobal Collection:** Danjaq / Eon / UA. Ph: Keith Hamshere (c). **112 Alamy Images:** RIA Novosti (clb). **The Kobal Collection:** Constantin-Bavaria-Wdr / Warner Bros (c); ITV Global. Ph: George Cannon (cl); Dreamworks (bc). **112-113 The Kobal Collection:** New Line Cinema (c). **113 Alamy Images:** Photos 12 / © 2009 Disney (crb); Photos 12 (cra). **114 Alamy Images:** Photos 12 / © 2010 Disney (bl). **© Disney:** Leah Gallo (tr). **The Kobal Collection. 114-115 The Kobal Collection:** © 2010 Disney (bc). **115 The Kobal Collection:** © 2010 Disney (tr, tl). **116 Alamy Images:** AF archive (cr); AF archive / © 2004 Disney / Pixar (bc). **The Kobal Collection:** Warner Bros / DC Comics (tl); Warner Bros. / DC Comics (clb). **117 The Kobal Collection: Columbia / © Marvel © 2013 CPII (r)**; Warner Bros. (bl). **118 The Kobal Collection:** Paramount / Rafran (crb); Warner Bros (bl). **Rex Features:** United Artists / Everett Collection (cra). **119 Alamy Images:** Photos 12 (cb). **The Kobal Collection:** Orion (bl); Universal (tr, crb). **120 Alamy Images:** Everett Collection Historical (bl). **Corbis:** Hemis / Escudero Patrick (cl). **The Kobal Collection:** 20th Century Fox (br). **121 Alamy Images:** Photos 12 (b). **The Kobal Collection:** 20th Century Fox (tl); Paramount (cr); Warner Bros. / Silver Pictures (br). **122 The Kobal Collection:** Block 2 Pics / Jet Tone (bl); Produzioni De Sica (cl); Universal (cr); Paramount (clb). **123 The Kobal Collection:** Legende / TFI International (tr); Working Title / Focus / Universal / StudioCanal. Ph: Alex Bailey (b). **124 The Kobal Collection:** Icon Entertainment (tc); ITV Global (c). **124-125 The Kobal Collection:** 20th Century Fox. Ph: Andrew Cooper (bc). **125 Getty Images:** (tr). **The Kobal Collection:** Orion (tl). **126 Alamy Images:** Photos 12 (cla). **The Kobal Collection:** Columbia (bl, cr); United Artists (tr); Touchstone. Ph: Richard Cartwright (crb). **127 The Kobal Collection:** Melodrama Pictures (tr); Pathé (b). **128 Alamy Images:** AF archive (tc, clb); Photos 12 (cla, bc). **The Kobal Collection:** Corona / Gibe / Selenia (cr). **129 Alamy Images:** Photos 12 (tl). **The Kobal Collection:** Cady / Discina / Specta (b). **130 The Kobal Collection:** MGM. Ph: C.S. Bull (c); United Artists (bl). **130-131 The Kobal Collection:** Warner Bros. / Silver Pictures (bc). **131 The Kobal Collection:** Miramax. Ph: Ricco Torres (tl); Universal (cr). **132 Alamy Images:** BP46C0 (tc). **132-133 The Kobal Collection:** Danjaq / Eon / UA (bc). **133 The Kobal Collection:** Columbia / Danjaq / Eon (cr); Danjaq / Eon / UA (tl, cra); Danjaq / Eon / UA. Ph: Keith Hamshere (c). **134 Alamy Images:** AF archive (cra). **The Kobal Collection:** GPO Film Unit (c); NFBC (cl); Maya Deren / Alexander Hammid (bc). **Rex Features:** Curzon / Everett Collection (br). **135 Alamy Images:** AF archive (cra). **The Kobal Collection:** Kanoon (tl); Optimum Productions (b). **136-137 Dreamstime.com:** Piotr Adamowicz. **136 Getty Images:** Steve Wisbauer (crb). **137 Getty Images:** Rana Faure (br). **Photo courtesy of Film Nation UK:** (tl, tc)

All other images © Dorling Kindersley
For further information see: www.dkimages.com

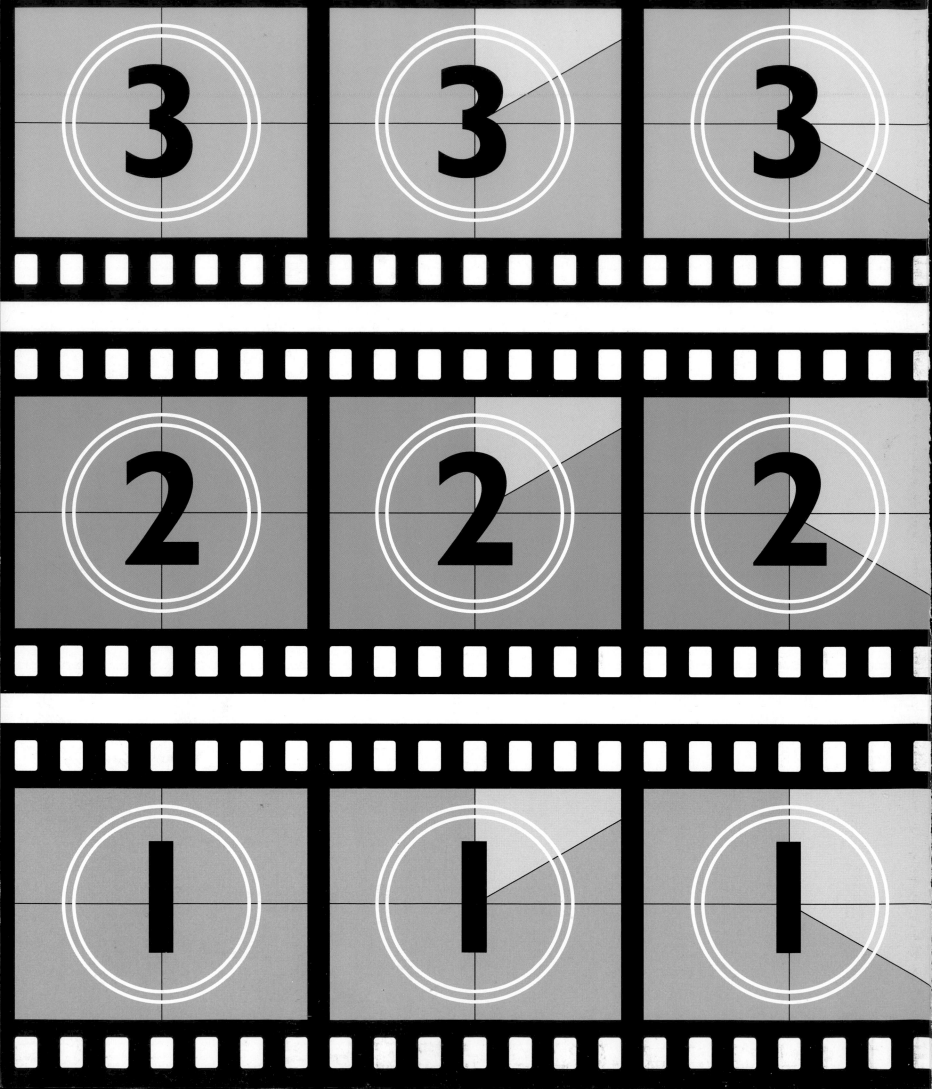